A RANCHER AND A WARRIOR:

THE LIFE OF DALE ROBINSON IN WYOMING AND WWII

By Jessica Robinson

Cover Design by AG
Edited by Lauren Jones, Turning Another page

ISBN-13: 978-1537756370
ISBN-10: 1537756370

INTRODUCTION

The following is the story of Dale's life as relayed to me through recordings and in-person interviews. In August 2014, he was interviewed by David E. Hillcurt of the Army Center of Military History. The interview lasted for more than 7 hours, and that audio is archived at the Army Center of Military History. The main topic of that conversation was about Dale's military service, and those interviews helped inform this book, but there is more material than I could incorporate.

The American Heritage Center (AHC) at the University of Wyoming has scanned copies of the scrapbook Dale's mother put together while he was overseas during WWII. It is part of a collection that honors and pays tribute to Wyoming veterans that served in various wars. It is available to the public. Many of the photos from that collection have been incorporated into this book. There are also photos from other collections that are housed at the AHC, and these are noted in the photo captions. The number at the end of the captions is the photo identifier, so if anyone is interested in finding a specific photo to get your own copy, this makes it easy.

This narrative is not an exhaustive chronicle of Dale's life but rather select stories and events that I thought best represented Dale as a person and highlighted his contributions to ranching, his country, and the world. Others may not agree with me, and that's fine. Dale—the only person whose opinion matters with this book—has approved the content.

When it was first suggested that Dale have a book written about his life, he wasn't too keen on the idea. He didn't think he had done anything worth talking about. Post-traumatic Stress Disorder (PTSD) also played a major role in that decision. Dale was unable to talk about his time in the war, which was an important part of the book. As time went on and Dale received better treatment for his PTSD, the idea of a biography became more appealing. His friends and family also played a role in convincing him to share his life in book form.

I was asked to take on this project for several different reasons. The first being that I am a published author. While I have never done a biography before this one, I have written nonfiction books, and through my day jobs I have had experience interviewing people and writing profiles. Secondly, I am Dale's granddaughter-in-law, and I was more than happy to help him tell his story.

This book is a celebration of Dale's life and the contributions he made to his country, science, and the world. Historical facts have been placed in the text to give context to his actions and deeds and to place them in the grander scheme of things. I hope you enjoy reading about Dale Robinson's life.

ACKNOWLEDGEMENTS

Several people have contributed to the creation of this book, and both Dale and I thank them from the bottom of our hearts. Many of them are listed below, but those who aren't, know that we appreciate everything you've done to help get this book completed.

Ade Peterson – thank you for taking the time to record your dad's stories and reminisce about the past. Without them, this book wouldn't have been written. Thank you also for recognizing the historic importance of Dale's scrapbook and making it available for all to see and enjoy.

Steve Elson – without your friendship and tireless effort to get Dale the recognition he deserves for what he did in WWII, this book probably wouldn't exist. You have gone above and beyond getting Dale recognized as the hero he is.

Dr. Bill Pickett – thank you for taking the time to meet with me and share your amazing stories about Dale and Jayne, along with the work that was accomplished in artificial insemination on his ranch. Again, I apologize for being late.

Dr. George Seidel – a thank you to you also for taking the time to speak to me about Dale's contribution to cattle reproductive science.

Dr. Jim Waggoner – thank you for sharing stories about Dale and molasses and the weight experiments that were conducted on the ranch.

Rick Ewig and the American Heritage Center – thank you for taking an interest in Dale's life and for making the scrapbook available for viewing for this generation and future generations.

Dr. Gregory Davis, Phoenix VA Psychiatrist – Dr. Davis, you must be one of the most unusual and best psychiatrists anywhere. You are completely different from other psychiatrists who told me such things as "You loved to kill Germans," when in fact I didn't. All they talked about was war and the very situations that upset me. From day one, you talked about everything but war and PTSD. I was confused by your talking about families, literature, music, comedy, art, sociology, and the breakdown of the American family due to the Interstate Highway system. It took me quite a while and talking with a friend to understand what you were doing—coming in the backdoor, so to speak, and preventing me from having a PTSD episode. I have never heard of a psychiatrist using your methods. THEY WORKED! I understood that your duties were primarily supervisory: teaching and monitoring other psychiatrists. I, who would literally break down with severe PTSD symptoms at the very mention of WWII, could not discuss my horrible experiences, the suffering and death, the loss of my men/friends, and the horrible cold of the Ardennes forest. Through a stroke of luck and with the help of a wonderful lady, I was able to bypass the VA bureaucracy and avoid another traumatic experience with VA psychiatrists who had brought on night terrors, walking in circles in the dark, and night sweats. Though you had every Wednesday as your administrative day, you sacrificed your time to treat me for one hour on a Wednesday morning. We bonded immediately; you are a truly unique and amazing person. Then, you agreed to see me for several more Wednesdays for one hour plus each. After less than 10 hours total, the terrors, shakes, tears, and nightmares disappeared. You, Dr. Davis, literally turned me from a shaking, teary-eyed, purplish hulk at the very mention of the War to a man who sat down with a representative from the Center for Military History (CMH in Washington, D.C.) and talked on tape for seven hours. The only applicable description of what happened is literally a miracle. You essentially cured me of the horrible effects of PTSD. No drugs, no marijuana, no shock treatments—simply a brilliant mind, UNcommon sense, and CARING ATTITUDE! GOD BLESS YOU, DR. GREGORY DAVIS!

Mr. L. W. Bailey, Wheat Farmer/Rancher (deceased) – I am grateful for the confidence and trust Mr. Bailey showed me at a very young age; he trusted the management of his entire ranch to me, Dale Robinson, in my early 20's. He gave me free reign to run all aspects of the ranch as I saw fit. It is rare to find such a person as Mr. Bailey who has complete trust even in those deserving of that trust. I never heard a single negative word about any person from or about Mr. Bailey. Mr. Bailey is a true gentleman who wore decency like a suit. The trust he placed in me did more for my self-esteem and confidence (excepting my parents) than any other person I have known. Mr. Bailey became my second dad; he treated me as one of his own.

I give credit to my parents, my wife, and Mr. Bailey for helping shape my life and giving me the confidence to succeed and accomplish things I didn't know I could do. Mr. Bailey was important in helping me separate things important from things superfluous.

TABLE OF CONTENTS

Page

INTRODUCTION i

ACKNOWLEDGEMENTS...iii

CHAPTER 1: THE RANCHING DREAM 1

CHAPTER 2: BASIC TRAINING 16

CHAPTER 3: THE JOURNEY OVERSEAS 29

CHAPTER 4: THE BATTLE OF THE BULGE 47

CHAPTER 5: ACTS OF HEROISM 62

CHAPTER 6: COMING HOME 76

CHAPTER 7: LIFE ON THE RANCH 90

CHAPTER 8: L.W. BAILEY 101

CHAPTER 9: ADVANCING THE SCIENCE OF

RANCHING 115

CHAPTER 10: LIFE AFTER THE RANCH 129

WORKS CITED 140

BIBLIOGRAPHY 150

.

Lance Dale Robinson, circa 1942 (courtesy of the American Heritage Center, ah12622_1_1).

CHAPTER 1:

THE RANCHING DREAM

Lance "Dale" Robinson had a dream—to one day own his own ranch. Born and raised in McFadden, Wyoming, ranching was all he'd ever known and all he wanted to do. Like many before him, Dale wanted to be part of the Wyoming tradition. Agriculture, second to energy development, had long been one of the main income producers for the state.

At first, Wyoming was just a place to pass through.[1] It wasn't until the late 1850s/early 1860s that people began to realize that the native grasses would be an excellent source of food for their livestock. Long before cattle ranchers came to the state, buffalo, elk, deer, antelope, and wild horses all survived on the grasslands that covered the land. It was the Civil War that changed how Wyoming was used. With Texas ranchers being cut off from eastern and southern markets and needing a place to graze their herds, they pushed them into Wyoming and Montana.[1] Grazing land here was "free" because it was still unclaimed by the public domain. And there were *thousands* of square miles. Once the transcontinental railroad was finished in 1869, ranchers had easy and rapid access to the eastern markets, making Wyoming and other western states the ideal place to make a fortune in the cattle business.

Wyoming became a territory in 1868, and in the 1870 census, there were 9,118 residents, with the majority of them in Cheyenne or Laramie and a few other railroad towns.[2] Even with the 1862 Homestead Act, which allowed homesteaders to claim 160 acres, the region was wide open, and that was what was appealing to cattlemen.

Without fences, cattle mixed with other herds on the open range. During the winter, most ranchers didn't feed their herd, relying on the land to take care of them, but in the spring, they had to round up their animals and mark the calves with their brands.[3] For small operations, this was a quick job, but for larger ranches, this could take months.

The cattle industry boomed, and it attracted wealthy individuals and investment companies from the East Coast, Scotland, and Britain.[4] Everyone was eager to make their fortunes on the Wyoming plains. And for a while, they did. Cheyenne became the home of many of these millionaires, and at one point, "various sources claimed that it was the wealthiest city per capita in the world."[4] The Union Pacific Railroad also helped build Cheyenne, and it became a major shipping point to send cattle back East.

Cattle and men flocked here in droves, and they made good money. Unfortunately, it didn't last long. In the winter of 1886-1887, there was a horrific snowstorm that killed many cattle. The storm raged for 72 hours, and temperatures dipped dangerously below zero.[5] The devastation wasn't discovered until spring. Carcasses were spread across fields and washed down streams. Those that had survived were emaciated and suffering from frost bite.[5] This led to poor market prices and the reorganization of the cattle industry. No longer were cattle grazing freely on the open range. Barbed wire fences were erected to keep them safe and within watering and feeding distance of the ranch. Many ranchers lost their fortunes and were forced out of Wyoming. The ones that faired the best were the small family operations, and many of them have been in operation for generations.[6]

Ranching in Wyoming still plays a major role. According to the U.S. Department of Agriculture National Agricultural Statistics Service, as of January 1, 2015, there were 1,300,000 cows, including calves, in Wyoming that were valued at $2.76 billion.[7]

The life of a cowboy is often romanticized, shown as a noble profession (which it is) full of pleasant nights under the stars and an exciting adventure of driving cattle across breathtaking landscapes. The reality was different, especially in the early days of cattle drives. Cowboys were exposed to all kinds of weather, from blazing hot to bitter cold and everything in between. Often they were without shelter, except for what they could carry on their saddles.

The land, while it could be scenic and beautiful, was also treacherous. Cattle drives could be thousands of miles long and there were rivers, mountains, and gullies that had to be crossed. Drives started shortly after dawn with a break at noon. On average, the group traveled 15 miles a day, and trips could take from 4 to 6 months to complete.[8] There could be thousands of cattle, but very few cowboys. An average drive consisted of a dozen cowboys, a trail boss, 50-60 horses, four mules, and a chuck wagon.[8] In addition to the land, there were also predators.

Cattlemen ventured west to make their fortunes in cattle, and many of them did, but that didn't always find its way down to the help. A cowboy's pay was often low, about $30 a month, unless they were a foreman, then they could earn $125.[9]

Cattle drives in this manner continued until the open range was fenced. Cowboys didn't have to drive cattle across the land, and technology eased some of their duties, which led to unemployment. The few who could still find work weren't paid overly well, but room and board was included in their wages and most large ranch operations had bunkhouses for their hands.

Their jobs demanded the attention of the ranch hands at least 6 days a week, usually before the sun rose until after it set. Rain or shine, the cowboy tends to his livestock.

Cattle in Wyoming, circa 1910-1915 (courtesy of the American Heritage Center, ah10472_0784).

Cowboys on the Wyoming range (courtesy of the American Heritage Center, ah01053_1463).

Postcard showing cattle on a river in Wyoming, circa 1906-1914 (courtesy of the American Heritage Center, ah10472_1336).

Cowboy branding calves (courtesy of the American Heritage Center, ah01053_1460).

Cattle round-up (courtesy of the American Heritage Center, ah05195_0128).

Postcard showing cowboys at dinner, circa 1906-1914 (courtesy of the American Heritage Center, ah10472_1392).

Dale was no stranger to the challenges that came with being a cowboy. Later in his life, when he returned to Wyoming after being in the war, he worked for a rancher from Cheyenne in the Wheatland Canyon area. He was low on funds at the time and living out of his car. On one particularly cold and snowy day, he had to gather the cows from Wheatland Canyon. As he was heading back with a calf slung across his saddle, the owner pulled up. It didn't escape Dale's notice how warm the car was, even though he could barely see through the snow that pelted him in the face. The owner asked how it was going, and Dale told him. Shortly after that, Dale turned in his resignation and looked for employment elsewhere.

Despite the hardship and long hours, ranching is an important part of Wyoming's economy and what Dale wanted to do. When he was a child, his father and Lloyd Dixon, a local rancher in the area, put him on the path to be successful in ranching. He had a typical ranch childhood and learned a lot about life and being a Wyoming rancher.

Dale was born on June 4, 1925, to Lance and Mary Robinson in McFadden, Wyoming. The town was established after the Ohio Oil Company bought a well in 1918 on the Cooper Ranch, which was approximately 12 miles southwest of Rock River, Wyoming.[10] Originally, the town was known as "Ohio City," then in 1920, it was changed to McFadyen after John "Uncle Jack" McFadyen, who was the Rocky Mountain general manager and later vice president for the Ohio Oil Company.[10] Later, it was changed to McFadden.

The town was built on top of a ridge, and the original structures were tar paper houses, a cook house, two schools, and a community center. These had no indoor plumbing. It wasn't until 1941 that the tar paper shacks were replaced with modern houses that had electricity, indoor plumbing and central heating.

His grandparents had settled in the area around Garrett, Wyoming, and his mom and dad met because of the nearness of their family ranches. It was a common occurrence among ranch families because of the isolation and unavailability of motor vehicles to take them to larger towns. Ranches were—and still are—passed down from one generation to the next, and whole regions could be controlled by multiple generations of one family.

With Wyoming being the least populated state in the nation and ranching as a major source of income, the rural way of life is all that a lot of people have known and, as believed by Dale, the only one worth living. The families in the area often got together and held dances. They were a tight-knit community that worked and played together. Lance and Mary met at one of these dances, married and started a family.

Even though McFadden had a company clinic to take care of the sick and injured, Dale was born on the ranch with his aunt in attendance as midwife. He was the youngest of two children. His brother was 16 months older than Dale.

Like most kids, Dale and Herb (his biological brother) would find ways to get in trouble. One particular occasion occurred when Dale was 6 or 7. He and his friends had taken up smoking and were near some trees enjoying a cigarette at school. The principal noticed the smoke and thought something was on fire, so went to put it out. When he realized it was the Robinson boys and a friend, he grabbed the paddle, the Bone Breaker, and gave them all a whack. Dale wasn't about to let his father know what had happened at school. Lance had told him that if he got into trouble there, he would also get more whacks at home. Dale felt the punishment from the Bone Breaker was sufficient.

Dale was just an occasional smoker in his younger years, but he had a friend who was a heavy smoker. Since none of them were old enough to buy cigarettes, they had to acquire them in other ways, which usually meant stealing from their parents. Dale often took packs out of his father's carton to give to his friend. They got caught once, but the punishment wasn't as harsh as they thought it would be. And they never stole any again.

Dale (center) with his mother and brother Herb, circa 1927 (courtesy of the American Heritage Center, ah12622_1_1).

Dale and Herb with Grandma Roe, taken July 1929 (courtesy of the American Heritage Center, ah12622_1_1).

Herb (left) and Dale, ages 13 and 11 (courtesy of the American Heritage Center, ah12622_1_1).

Board with a list of names outside of McFadden school (courtesy of the American Heritage Center, ah12622_1_1).

What is left of the McFadden school, 2015 (taken by Jessica Robinson).

Dale and Herb eventually got caught smoking by their father, and Dale thought for sure the punishment was going to be severe. Instead, Lance invited both boys into the house with a smile. Lance set up three chairs in front of a long, 6-ft mirror that was hung by the door. He gave them cigarettes out of his pack, and they all lit up. They smoked and laughed and had a great time. Dale was relieved that nothing worse had happened. But after three puffs, Dale started crying and threw his away.

"I just wanted you boys to see how you looked smoking a cigarette at your age," Lance said.

And Dale noticed it. At that moment, he decided it was time to quit.

Dale always had a great relationship with his parents. He often thought of them more as his best friends than his mom and dad. Later in life, one of the favorite pastimes of father and son was to head to Wendover for relaxation and gambling.

The town of Wendover straddles the Utah/Nevada border, and West Wendover, which is in Nevada, has legalized gambling.[11] Development of the town began in the 1930s and 1940s. At the time, a small cobblestone service station was erected that provided a place for weary travelers to rest. In the 1970s and 1980s, the town grew as a destination resort. More business and casinos moved in, along with hotels and other service establishments. It has thrived as a gambling town and generated tax revenue for city services and better schools. West Wendover isn't a large town. The 2010 census claims that it had a population of 4,410. The 2000 census showed it had 4,721 people living in the city limits.[11]

Interestingly, Wendover, Utah, played a major role in WWII. During the late 1930s, Wendover Field was conceived, and in 1940, Congress appropriated funds for the acquisition of land for bombing and gunnery ranges.[12] This particular location was chosen because of its closeness to the Great Salt Lake desert and vast uninhabited terrain. At the time, the city was populated with 103 people and had railroad lines that ran between Salt Lake City and three West Coast cities.

The first unit assigned to Wendover Field moved in on August 12, 1941. The Wendover Army Air Base was activated on March 28, 1942, as a B-17 and B-24 bombardment base. The first unit was the 306th bombardment group with four squadrons that arrived in mid-April 1942.[12]

Training at the base included high-altitude formation flying, long-range navigation, target identification, and simulated combat missions. In the end, 21 bomber groups and more than 1,000 aircrews completed their training at Wendover Airfield. The soldiers played different roles in the war, including being part of the strategic bombing of Germany, air support for D-Day, and other combat operations around the world.[12]

The field played other important roles, including being the base for a group of officials that worked on "Project W-47," a key part of the Manhattan Project. Bombs were assembled there, and groups left the base to destinations all over the world for various missions. Immediately after the war, the unit that had been stationed at Wendover was transferred to another base, along with all of the nuclear bomb tooling. By 1946, nothing was left at Wendover base.[12]

But that wasn't the area Dale and his father visited. They went to the "fun" Wendover in Nevada. Apparently, Lance was a bit of a tightwad—until they got to Wendover, then he loosened up. He was also often incredibly lucky and went home with more than he came with. He enjoyed the slot machines while Dale took his chances at the tables. They had a system worked out for when Lance needed money so he wouldn't disturb Dale. He would walk into the room and say "Shoosh!" Hearing the sound, Dale would hold up a bill that his father would take, and they would both continue their games. Often, Dale would be so focused on his game, he wouldn't pay attention to how many times his father called out, and Lance used that to his advantage. He would get money from Dale when he wasn't out. But he was always willing to share his winnings.

On one particular trip, Lance and Jayne had just *shooshed* some bills from Dale and were headed to the slot machines to play. Lance normally played the $1 slots, but every machine was full. The only two that were open were $5 machines, so he figured, *What the hell?* He inserted his money and pulled the handle. Jackpot! Jayne then went to the second machine and repeated the action. Jackpot! Everyone went home a little richer and happier at the end of the trip.

Family has always been important to Dale, including extended family, and he always tried to help out when he could. After he married, he and his wife would go to California to visit her parents and he would always give them cash before leaving. On one occasion, he bought them a car. It made him happy to know he could help.

But most of this happened much later in Dale's life—after he had grown up and come back from the war. His life on the ranch was pretty typical. He worked hard and learned what it took to be successful. They were skills that would serve him well when he was called upon to serve his time in WWII. Before heading to basic training, Dale needed some funds, so he got them the easiest way he could: skinning cows.

Skinning animals was a skill that helped Dale all throughout his childhood and allowed him to earn extra cash. In addition to cattle, he would also skin beaver, a skill that was taught to him by another rancher. This rancher taught him a special way to cut the feet so he always knew which beaver pelts were his. Only Dale and this guy cut them in this way so no one else could steal their hides. What he was paid for each pelt depended on the market, but he had received $60 per pelt at one time.

When it came to skinning cows, Lloyd Dixon, the ranch owner Dale worked for, would let him know where a lost cow was located—and when he said "lost," he meant a cow that had died of natural causes. Dale would head to it and remove the hide. He usually rode a horse to the site, which was problematic because it was hard for him to get the hide and himself on the saddle. The horses didn't like the hide draped across them. His dad told him about an old Model A on the property and gave Dale permission to take it, so he did. He learned how to skin cows fast. He would start by taking the legs out and then part of the sides, then he would hook onto the head with the Model A and take off for home. The hide would come right off the carcass.

Cow hides didn't go for as much as beaver pelts, usually only about $4 or $5 a piece, but Dale made $180 to take with him to the Army. His father recommended that he only take half, and Dale heeded his advice. Armed with $90 and a sense of duty, Dale left the ranch and McFadden to set the world right.

Lloyd Dixon in 1942 (courtesy of the American Heritage Center, ah12622_1_1).

CHAPTER 2:

BASIC TRAINING

When Dale was 10, he took a job at a local pig farm as the cook's assistant. His duties required him to be up before everyone else so that he could make sure the table was set and everyone was fed. The cooks weren't always the nicest people, and on more than one occasion, Dale stormed off from his job, intent on never returning. More often than not, his father would march him back to the farm to continue his duties. He was told that he couldn't quit until the end of the season, and his dad wasn't going to let him quit every job he started.

The situation with the cooks often didn't get better when he returned. Since they knew Dale was stuck, they often worked him that much harder. However, Dale learned valuable lessons. The experience instilled in him a work ethic and sense of duty, and it taught him how to take orders—a trait that came in handy when he joined the Army.

Dale was 16 years old when Pearl Harbor was bombed, and like every other boy in the country, he wanted his chance to prove his patriotism and defend democracy against the tyranny that threatened to take over the world. His brother was already in the Navy, and Dale waited impatiently for his chance to enlist.

The bombing of Pearl Harbor on December 7, 1941, by Japanese fighters marked America's commitment to join WWII. Before this incident, they tried to maintain a neutral position, even though they supplied weapons, ships, planes, and ammunition to Britain to help them fight the Germans.

After Pearl Harbor, the U.S. committed to send soldiers over to fight the war.

Dale was more than willing to do his part, but enlisting in the Army was a bit problematic. For starters, Dale was in agriculture, and his services would be more beneficial at home. Not willing to take no as an answer, he left ranching and took a job as a welder. That accomplished the goal. On August 9, 1943, Dale enlisted in the Army. He was barely 18. Dale was eager to get where the action was and "be one of the boys." One of his friends that he had gone to school with in McFadden also enlisted.

He left from Rawlins on an old bus to go to Denver. At that point, he was kind of scared—both of what he was getting into and because he wasn't sure the bus would actually make it. Many of the other recruits were also feeling the anxiety. The vast majority of them had never left home. But that didn't concern Dale. He had always been independent and worked away from home since he was 10. But there was still a concern of what lay ahead. Thankfully, the bus ride came with entertainment.

One of the fellow recruits was a bit of a jokester. On the way to Denver, as they passed through towns, he would holler out the windows at the girls. When they got to Denver, they were immediately lined up for a health inspection. The jokester stood in front of the doctor, who also happened to be a captain, and was told, "Skin her back and milk her down."

To which he replied, "Doc, just smile at it, it'll skin itself back."

All the recruits thought the remark was funny, but no one dared laugh. It was obvious that the captain didn't see the humor in his words. The funny man was court martialed after only being enlisted for 2 days. He was the example that the Army wasn't going to tolerate any shenanigans, and the others fell in line. Dale certainly didn't want to have to explain to his parents that he got in trouble, so he straightened up instantly and prepared to follow orders.

No doubt the soldier's sarcastic reaction to the situation was driven by fear of the unknown. Dale certainly felt it. After passing the initial examination, they were fed, issued uniforms, and assigned to barracks. There was very little time for anything, and the new recruits were expected to change quickly into their new attire and prepare for drills. Dale had no idea what was going on, so his fear was renewed. He changed as quickly as he could, throwing his belongings onto his bed, including all the money he had. When he returned later, the money was gone. Someone made out really well that day going through the new recruits' belongings. A few of the soldiers sat down on the bed and began to cry, but Dale let his anger lead the way. He asked to see the colonel, and he was taken into his office.

"What are you here for, soldier?" the colonel asked.

"Somebody stole my money," Dale explained.

"They did?"

"Yes, they did."

"How much did you have?"

Dale told him.

"You sit down right there and I'll get you a pencil and paper and you give me those serial numbers and I'll have that money back to you before the night."

At this point, Dale's anger and agitation was growing, and he didn't hide his contempt. "Come on!" he huffed. "What do you think you're doing? Give me the number of your bills."

The colonel's patience and friendly demeanor was wearing thin. "Don't get smart with me, soldier. You're in the Army now, and I can't do anything for you unless you can give me the serial numbers."

Dale knew there was nothing more that could be done, so he walked out of the office angry. It was an encounter that would always stick with him and sour his perception of the Army.

Dale was a member of the 313th Infantry, Company H. According to the history[1], the infantry was activated on June 15, 1942. The staff were appointed as follows:

Executive Officer: Colonel Charles W. Hanna
Adjutant: Captain Phil Lofink
Intelligence Officer: 1st Lieutenant Frederick L. Grant
Plans & Training: Major Clair B. Mitchell
Supply Officer: Captain Steward Lawrence

The regiment was commanded by Colonel Paul C. Paschal. He had attended the United States Military Academy at West from 1910 to 1914; the Infantry School at Fort Benning, Georgia, in 1923; the Command and General Staff School, Fort Leavenworth, Kansas, in 1924; and the Army War College, Washington, D.C., during 1928 and 1929. The assignments he was given afterward were also noteworthy:

He was appointed to the War Department General Staff for a term extending from 1931 to 1935. Transferred from there to The Infantry School, Fort Benning, Georgia, in 1913, he served as an instructor until 1939. Following this he was assigned as instructor at The Army War College, Washington, D.C. Shortly thereafter, during 1940 and 1941, he served as Commanding Officer of the 38th Infantry. From there he returned to teaching, having been assigned to the Reserve Officers Training Corps, University of Kentucky, as Professor of Military Science and Tactics.[2]

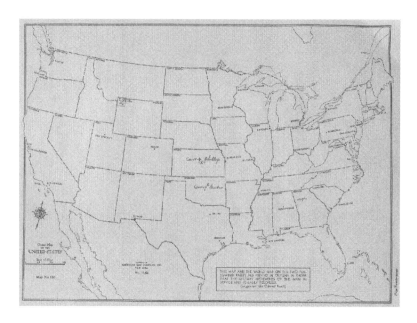

Map from Dale's war scrapbook. His mom marked where his basic training camps were located (courtesy of the American Heritage Center, ah12622_1_1).

Although Dale doesn't remember the specifics of who was in charge of his unit after all these years, and probably didn't realize it at the time, he was a member of a unit that would accomplish many great victories in the war. But before heading overseas, Dale had to complete his training in the U.S.

After Denver, Dale was sent to basic training at Camp Gruber near Muskogee, Oklahoma.[3] It was located on Highway 10, 18 miles east of Muskogee. This camp was constructed in response to the U.S.'s commitment to war. Construction began in February 1942 with a work force of 12,000 men. "The production pace in the first month was so hectic that a building was completed every twenty minutes, twenty-four hours a day, seven days a week. It took four months to build the camp, at a project cost of thirty million dollars."[3]

The main post occupied 260 acres with 2,250 buildings. There was a 1,600-bed hospital, 479 barracks, 19 post exchanges, 12 chapels, and various social and recreations centers. There was also a central post office with three branches. This camp had become a city within itself.

The parade ground was nearly 2 miles in length, and barracks lined one side. Built off the ground, the barracks were painted white with green trim. Some of the other buildings on the base had concrete foundations. There were gravel sidewalks that linked the buildings, and streets within the main post were paved. Camp Gruber had a bus service to provide transportation within the camp. The cost was 5 cents. There was even a rail system that extended into the post so that loading and unloading of troops and supplies could be done with ease.

Entertainment at Camp Gruber was also a priority, and there were three swimming pools, a sports arena, and 24 softball and 10 baseball diamonds. There were restrictions on hunting at Camp Gruber, but fishing was allowed at nearby Greenleaf Lake. There were theaters that brought the latest films to the soldiers, and four theaters in the large auditoriums sat more than 900 people. The camp provided boxing matches and USO shows for special entertainment.

Dale never spoke of participating in any of these events while at Camp Gruber. He may not remember them happening or was possibly not there long enough to utilize these amenities. Either way, it was a large camp that played a major role in preparing soldiers for the war.

In 1943, Camp Gruber became a POW camp.[3] It had the capacity to hold 5,750 prisoners, and branches were located at Bixby, Haskell, Morris, Okemah, Okmulgee, Porter and Wetumka. Camp Gruber only housed German captives, and the first prisoners of war were received May 29, 1943. The prisoner compound was closed in May 1946. The highest number of POWs held at the camp was 4,702. But that was long after Dale had spent time at the camp.

When Dale's time there was done, he moved on to the next assignment. From Camp Gruber, he went to Camp Phillips.[4] This camp was built to be a large-scale military training camp. It grew to more than 46,000 acres and housed 75,000 to 80,000 soldiers at one time. Designed to be a 5-year camp, it also served as a POW camp for 3,000 Germans and Italians. Close by, Schilling Air Force Base was built at the same time.

Time has taken many of the names of Dale's fellow soldiers and his commanding officers from his memory, but according to the *History of the 313th Infantry in World War II*[5], a major party was tasked with preparing Camp Phillips for the 313th's arrival. It consisted of Major Phil Lofink, Captain Thomas L. Lyons, Lieutenant Curtis V. Blakely, Lieutenant Virgil D. Basinger, CWO Jinks N. Durden, and 33 enlisted men. Their task of preparing the camp for the men's arrival was done smoothly and quickly, so when the troops arrived, everything was ready for them.

Although Dale doesn't talk about it, the soldiers at Camp Phillips had a grand social life.[6] Dinners and dances were held quite often for the men to partake in. Rest and relaxation were just as important to the Army as drills, and it helped with morale. After all, these young men were expected to head overseas and fight in a war—perhaps give their lives for their country. It was a scary time, but an active social life helped keep their mind off their impending destiny and their fighting spirits up.

Part of Dale's military training involved long hikes—sometimes up to 60 miles—in preparation for the fighting that would occur overseas. He and his fellow soldiers were often required to carry their field packs on these excursions, and Dale lamented how heavy they were. He spent some time in the kitchens during training and noticed large gallon food cans. He realized that stacking two on top of one another and then covering it with a blanket made it immensely lighter than his field pack, and it still carried the essentials. He took his invention out on several hikes, and his fellow comrades noticed how much easier of a time he was having and requested cans of their own. Several of them used this lighter contraption for a while, but the closer the troops got to being deployed, the less they were allowed to use them. Eventually, they had to go back to the Army-issued packs.

Dale's time in training was often uneventful, mainly because he didn't want to have to explain to his parents why he got into trouble—if he were to—but there were some things he was particular about. He could be stubborn and outspoken. One such occasion involved a haircut. It occurred on the parade grounds, and Dale got into an argument with another noncommissioned officer. At the time, Dale had been a corporal. The other soldier told him he needed to get a haircut.

"I know I need a haircut," Dale responded. "And I will when we're not restricted to the area."

"Well, you got a company barber," the other soldier said.

"No, they're not a barber. They're just a junker. When I can go down to the PX where I can get a regular barber, I'll have my hair cut."

(The PX is a military store that sells discounted items to soldiers and their families.)

"I told you to get your hair cut right now. Somebody there can cut your hair. I don't care how it looks."

At this point, Dale was irritated, and he wasn't going to be pushed around. He told the man, "But I do! And I'm not gonna get my hair cut 'til I can go to the PX."

The other soldier's temper also flared. "Are you trying to get smart with me, soldier?"

"No, I'm not trying to do anything. Unless you want to."

"Well, how tough do you think you are?"

"I don't know." Dale laid his gun on the ground. "Let's see."

But the other soldier wasn't going to fight. He simply told Dale to get back in line, then dismissed everyone else but Dale. "See the captain."

Postcards sent home by Dale from Camp Phillips (courtesy of the American Heritage Center, ah12622_1_1).

Dale in the Army kitchens (courtesy of the American Heritage Center, ah12622_1_1).

Dale knew he was busted, and he headed in to see the captain.

"What's this I hear about you out on the parade ground?" the captain asked.

"I don't know," responded Dale. "I guess it's all true whatever you heard, so I'm not gonna change it."

"Well, I guess that's all I need then, *Private* Robinson."

And Dale's career as a corporal was cut short. However, he figured it would have been. When he wrote home to his parents, he never signed his letters as "corporal." He knew his mom would have been upset by what had happened and him being demoted. He figured she would have told him that she had raised him better.

Dale was trained as a heavy machine gunner. He used a Browning M2HB .50 caliber. He was also trained to use the .30 carbine and an M1 rifle, and he also carried a heavy Colt .45. Coming from a ranch and having hunted for most of his life, he was an expert shot. No doubt, this skill came in handy while he was overseas. And that fell right in line with the rest of his unit. According to the *History of the 313th Infantry in World War II*:

> The rifle firing while at Camp Phillips was carried out during the latter part of December and the month of January. Needless to say, the weather was much of the time intensely cold and the firing was often carried on under difficulty. Despite this, however, the 313th Infantry as a whole chalked up for itself one of the finest firing records for any Infantry outfit. The figures were almost unbelievable. Colonel Wood had set a goal for the men, stating that he would like to see every man in the Regiment qualify as either Sharpshooter or Expert. This was asking almost more than one could humanely hope to expect, for as a rule a regiment that can qualify every man as Marksman or better is doing a fine piece of work. Colonel Wood did not necessarily expect his men to achieve the goal he had set, but when the final figures were tallied, his goal was not far from having been reached. The final figures showed that 52 per cent of the Regiment had qualified as Sharpshooter, 32 per cent as Expert and 16 per cent as Marksman. Not a single man failed to qualify with a grade less than that of Marksman, and the high percentage of Sharpshooters and Experts was an amazing demonstration of shooting ability. Colonel Wood was more than pleased and so was the

Division commander, General Wyche. With a
record like that one set by the 313th Infantry,
there need be no fear of a good showing on the
field of battle.[7]

Despite the record the unit made in their shooting ability,
there were moments when the soldiers would have fun on the
shooting range. The field was set up with a series of targets on
berms with ditches in between. Soldiers that weren't firing
were sent out into the ditches between the berms with different
colored flags that indicated where on the target the shooter hit.
Due to the distance, the soldiers and the commanders in the
firing box relied on the soldiers in the ditches to give them an
accurate indication, but sometimes the soldiers just wanted to
have fun.

On one such occasion, Dale and his friends were in the
ditch and when the soldiers fired, even if they hit a bullseye,
they would hold up the flag that indicated they missed.

"We could hear the sergeants on the firing line take the rifle
and make adjustments," says Dale. "Then, the soldiers would
fire again and the shot would go sailing over the target, but we
indicated it was a bullseye."

Dale and his friends could barely contain their amusement.
It was a rare moment of goofing off. When the situation called
for seriousness, they were able to meet the challenge.

As a heavy machine gunner, Dale's role was to position
himself on the landscape so that he could shoot over his fellow
soldiers, taking out the enemy to keep them safe. He and his
assistant gunner were responsible for carrying the machine
gun, tripod, and extra ammunition—all of which easily
weighed more than 100 lbs. But Dale was young and eager to
defend his country, so it was a burden he was willing to bear.

After training in the U.S., it was time to head overseas.
With a sense of duty and all the courage he could muster, Dale
embarked on a life-changing journey.

Dale with his heavy machine gun (courtesy of the American Heritage Center, ah12622_1_1).

CHAPTER 3:

THE JOURNEY OVERSEAS

At this point, Dale had left the 313th and became part of the 79th Reconnaissance Troop. Dale left from Camp Phillips and headed to Camp Myles Standish. They traveled through New York at night, and Dale stayed awake to take in the sights. He had never been there and was interested to see what it looked like, and the view from the train window didn't disappoint. But on this trip, that was as much as he would experience of the Big Apple. In all the various places Dale had the opportunity to travel through, cities rarely held any interest to him. He'd never lived in one. What he found intriguing was the farming country he traveled through. This was something he was familiar with. But, with the task of preparing for war taking precedent, he never had time to indulge his curiosity about these new places.

They weren't at Camp Myles Standish long before they were loaded onto the *S.S. Strathmore* and headed for the journey overseas. In the *History of the 313th*, the ship is described as follows:

> By way of background, it will be of interest to know something of the size and history of the *Strathmore*. The *Strathmore*, a British steamer, was the thirteenth largest steamship in the world. She was a *de luxe* liner, owned by the Peninsular and Oriental Steam Ship Company, Ltd., which operated a regular passenger service between England and the Indies before the war.

She had a water displacement of 23,500 tons, and was first launched in 1936. When World War II began the *Strathmore* was immediately taken over by the British Government for use as a troopship, and had made many a voyage carrying British troops and supplies to combat areas. This was her first mission however, as a transport carrying American troops. She had made the voyage from Liverpool, England, to Boston Harbor without escort, and had been docked at Commonwealth Pier, Boston, for about ten days before the first American troops had boarded her. Now she was loaded to capacity with troops and equipment, ready to carry them to their unknown destination.[1]

Six thousand troops were loaded onto the ship, which had a normal capacity of 1,500 passengers. Every square inch of the vessel was put to use to accommodate either the troops or their equipment. Those aboard the *Strathmore* included: the 313th Infantry, 2d Battalion of the 314th Infantry, the 79th Reconnaissance Troop, the 310th Field Artillery, and 63 American nurses from the 4th Auxiliary Surgical Group.

Dale was placed on G Deck. Conditions were incredibly crowded, and the soldiers were expected to eat and sleep in their assigned areas. Dale was given the choice of getting a hammock or a mattress to sleep on. The mattresses were placed on the table tops, and the hammocks were hung. Dale decided he would take a hammock, thinking it would be more comfortable than the thin mattress he would be assigned. He quickly regretted his decision. He had never slept in a hammock before, and it was hung over his fellow soldiers. If the ship pitched sharply, he could be thrown out and onto a comrade in arms. But at that point, it was too late to change his mind.

The voyage didn't agree with Dale, and he spent the entire time sea sick. The swinging from the hammock didn't help much, so he had to find a place where he could get some rest. He found it underneath the stairs where he curled up to sleep. Thankfully, they didn't have anything to do on the ship—no training was conducted—with the exception of boat drills.

It was altogether impossible to plan any training while aboard ship. Even classroom instruction was discontinued for the duration of the voyage. The attention of officers in charge was directed solely toward the end of assuring safe crossing for all troops, and of keeping them occupied with diversionary interests while the voyage lasted. To insure a minimum loss of life in the event of disaster, daily boat drills were held. At 10:30 a.m. daily an alert was scheduled, and when the alarm sounded, all troops moved immediately to specified locations on upper decks. All troops, day and night, were required to wear life preservers. From the moment a soldier came aboard ship until he debarked the life preserver became a permanent part of his equipment. He was allowed to remove it only when sleeping, and even then, regulations required him to have it within immediate reach. This same rule applied to all officers and members of the ships' crew. After the troops became familiar with the boat-drill routine, a night drill was carried out. Under blackout conditions all troops were required to move to their stipulated places on the upper decks. In case the ship was torpedoed, it was explained, the lighting system would probably fail, and it was essential that the troops knew how to find their way to safety under conditions of total darkness. The troops learned quickly and willingly to comply with all regulations, and within a few days the drills were executed without any difficulty whatsoever.[2]

This was an important part of being on the ship in case submarines sank the boat. The men needed to know how to evacuate, which could potentially save their lives. Otherwise, the soldiers spent their time playing cards and dice. With the ship being as crowded as it was, there wasn't much else to do. At night, blackout conditions were enforced. No one was allowed to smoke on deck. It was so dark, Dale could barely see his hand in front of his face. This was important to keep the ship hidden from enemies as it headed toward England. German submarines were always on the lookout for ships to sink, and the *Strathmore* wanted to make it as difficult as possible for them.

After 14 days, the *Strathmore* finally docked in Scotland— at first it dropped anchor at the port of Grenock, then later headed to Glasgow, where it remained docked for 2 days before the troops were allowed to debark. From there, they headed to Liverpool, England, where they were housed in a tent city. Dale was surprised at how nice the tents and area were. Rock paths lined the area, keeping the soldiers out of mud when they entered and left their sleeping quarters. The latrine was situated a ways from the camp, and the area was kept clean and tidy. Dale noticed that many of the local farmers would come daily to clean out the latrines and used the waste as fertilizer for their crops. Shaking his head, he appreciated that they kept the area tidy, but he hoped he never had to resort to such methods on his ranch.

The troops participated in close-order drills and wall and rope ladder training. After a month, Dale and his fellow soldiers were ready for combat. The 79th unit was activated on June 15, 1942, and was sent overseas on April 7, 1944.[3] The commanders were as follows:

From June 1942-May 1945: Major General Ira T. Wyche
From May-July 1945: Brigadier General LeRoy H. Watson
From July-August 1945: Major General Anthony C. McAuliffe
From August 1945 to inactivation: Brigadier General LeRoy H. Watson

The following gives a brief account of the division's combat chronicle[3] (the paragraph breaks were added by the author):

> After training in the United Kingdom from 17 April 1944, the 79th Infantry Division landed on Utah Beach, Normandy, 12-14 June and entered combat 19 June 1944, with an attack on the high ground west and northwest of Valognes and high ground south of Cherbourg. The Division took Fort du Roule after a heavy engagement and entered Cherbourg, 25 June. It held a defensive line at the Ollonde River until 2 July 1944 and then returned to the offensive, taking La Haye du Puits in house-to-house fighting, 8 July.
>
> On 26 July, the 79th attacked across the Ay River, took Lessay, crossed the Sarthe River and entered Le Mans, 8 August, meeting only light resistance. The advance continued across the Seine, 19 August. Heavy German counterattacks were repulsed, 22-27 August, and the Division reached the Therain River, 31 August. Moving swiftly to the Franco-Belgian frontier near St. Amand, the Division encountered heavy resistance in taking Charmes in street fighting, 12 September. The 79th cut across the Moselle and Meurthe Rivers, 13-23 September, cleared

the Foret de Parroy in a severe engagement, 28 September-9 October, and attacked to gain high ground east of Embermenil, 14-23 October, when it was relieved, 24 October.

After rest and training at Luneville, the Division returned to combat with an attack from the Mignevine Montiguy area, 13 November 1944, which carried it across the Vezouse and Moder Rivers, 18 November-10 December, through Haguenau in spite of determined enemy resistance, and into the Siegfried Line, 17-20 December. The Division held a defensive line along the Lauter River, at Wissembourg from 20 December 1944 until 2 January 1945, when it withdrew to Maginot Line defenses. The German attempt to establish a bridgehead west of the Rhine at Gambsheim resulted in furious fighting. The 79th beat off German attacks at Hatten and Rittershoffen in an 11-day battle before withdrawing to new defensive positions south of Haguenau on the Moder River, 19 January 1945. The Division remained on the defensive along the Moder until 6 February 1945.

After resting in February and March 1945, the Division returned to combat, 24 March 1945, crossed the Rhine, drove across the Rhine-Herne Canal, 7 April, secured the north bank of the Ruhr and took part in clearing the Ruhr Pocket until 13 April. The Division then went on occupation duty, in the Dortmund, Sudetenland, and Bavarian areas successively, until its return to the United States and inactivation.[3]

The insignia of the division was the Cross of Lorraine, which was on a blue shield with a gray border. Dale's cross has been stored in the scrapbook his mother put together for him during his time in the war. In there is also the small booklet *The Cross of Lorraine Division: The story of the 79th*, which was published by the Stars & Stripes in Paris in 1944-1945. The booklet covered the history of the 79th Division, which had originally been mobilized in WWI.

The history of the 79th is long and detailed, but most of it doesn't pertain to Dale and his fellow soldiers. By the time he became a member, the division had been a skeleton crew that had to be built up from the bottom.

During WWII, Dale and the 79th's mission was to go to France and liberate the city of Cherbourg. This was an important task because Cherbourg was a port city that would allow the allies to get supplies into France and to the troops. It was also a staging point for the Germans to set up their large guns and shell Britain. Taking back Cherbourg would be a great victory for the Allies and stop the advance of the Germans into Europe. Dale and his unit of the 79th entered France 6 days after D-Day.

The Battle of Normandy lasted from June 1944 to August 1944 and liberated Western Europe from Nazi Germany's control.[4] The battle began on June 6, 1944, and had been codenamed "Operation Overlord," but was also known as D-Day. Approximately 156,000 American, British, and Canadian forces landed on five beaches along a 50-mile stretch of beach off France's Normandy coast. These beaches were heavily fortified with German forces. The D-Day invasion was one of the largest amphibious attacks in military history. The planning required to pull it off was extensive.

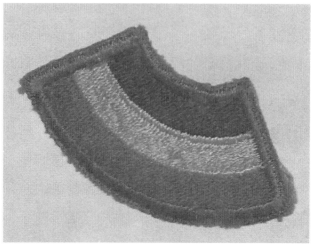

Dale's patches from the 79th Division (courtesy of the American Heritage Center, ah12622_1_1).

Copy of the history of the 79th Division that Dale sent home to his parents (courtesy of the American Heritage Center, ah12622_1_1).

One of the best tactics an army can use is the element of surprise. The goal is to catch the enemy unprepared and use it to gain a victory. While preparing for D-Day, the Allies set up a large-scale deception campaign to mislead the Germans on where their intended invasion targets were. Hitler had been aware that the Allies were planning an invasion, and he put one of his most trusted and victorious generals in charge of the defense operations. Erwin Rommel was charged with finishing the Atlantic Wall, which was a 24,000-mile fortification of bunkers, landmines, and beach and water obstacles.

The Allies continued with their deception campaign. They led the Germans to believe that the main invasion target was Pas-de-Calais, which was the narrowest point in the channel between Britain and France, and that Norway and a few other locations were potential invasion targets. They went so far as using fake equipment, a phantom army that was supposedly based in England, double agents, and fraudulent radio transmissions.

On June 6th by dawn, thousands of paratroopers and gilder troops had already descended to the ground behind enemy lines. Their job was to secure bridges and exit roads. The invasion from the channel began at 6:30 a.m. The British and Canadian forces were met with light opposition and captured the beaches code named Gold, Juno, and Sword. The Americans had the same luck at Utah Beach. Omaha Beach was a different story, and the Americans faced heavy resistance. More than 2,000 American soldiers lost their lives on that beach that day. In all, some estimates claim that more than 4,000 Allied soldiers died during the D-Day invasion, with thousands more wounded or missing. However, 156,000 Allied troops successfully stormed Normandy's beaches. On June 11, the beaches were fully secured. More than 326,000 troops, 50,000 vehicles, and 100,000 tons of equipment had landed at Normandy.

Surprise helped in the attack, along with the deception tactics, but the Germans were also experiencing confusion and were missing Rommel when the attacks started. Hitler believed that the first attacks were a feint. He believed the real attacks would be coming from north of the Seine River, so he refused to release nearby divisions as backup. He called reinforcements from further away, which caused delays. Allied air support also played a major role in hampering the Germans. They took out key bridges, forcing the German reinforcements to take long detours. Allied naval support also helped protect advancing Allied troops.

Dale entered France 6 days after the D-Day invasion by crossing the English Channel. Dale, along with the other soldiers, were crammed into a landing barge. He could barely breathe, let alone move. When the front of the barge opened, he and the other men ran to disembark. It was then that the war became real. Chest deep in water, with shells hitting the beach in front of them, Dale headed for his objective. Along the way, he had to push bodies out of the way and ships were upturned in the water around him. Every so often, he or a fellow soldier would step into a shell hole and disappear under the water, only to resurface a short time later, still running for the beach.

Carrying his .30 caliber, Dale stepped onto Utah Beach and made it as far on the beach as he could. Steep ridges lay before him. Soldiers were in chaos, running unorganized out of the water into the field of battle. But this situation was planned for. The commanders knew that the crossing would be chaotic and soldiers would get separated from their units, so they were trained how to identify themselves and regroup. As soon as Dale found his fellow soldiers, he dug a hole and awaited further orders.

Crossing the channel brought Dale in contact with Germans. Most of them were dead, but there were a few prisoners of war who were being led by Army Rangers. These Rangers were outnumbered by German prisoners 500 to 1, but not one of them dared step out of line. If they did, they were shot. Fear was a great motivator to keep them in line.

After passing by the Rangers, Dale noticed an old German sitting beneath a tree. The man had stopped to rest and smoke a pipe. Dale thought the man looked too old to be a soldier. As Dale looked at him, a shell came in and the shrapnel killed the man so fast, the pipe never fell out of his mouth. The reality of the situation settled on Dale, leaving him shaken and scared, but there was nothing he could do now but his job—and survive.

> Early on the morning of June 26 the Regiment smashed its way into Cherbourg. The 1st Battalion was on the right and the 2d Battalion was on the left. The order of the day was speed. There was considerable house-to-house fighting. Sniper fire was persistent. By 8:30 a.m. the leading elements had reached the water line and the rest of the day was spent in rounding up the scattered Germans who had been split into small groups by the rapidity of the advance. Hundreds were taken prisoner. Some German officers were acting as snipers and they had hid on the third floors of buildings. It took time to kill them.[5]

Cherbourg was in Allied control later that afternoon, and the men rested in the houses before heading out on June 27 for their next mission.

After taking Cherbourg, Dale and his unit continued through France. The land they traversed was called "hedgerow country," and fighting was difficult.[6] In France, farmland was separated by thick hedges. These hedges were so dense, Dale commented that a rabbit would have a hard time getting through the branches. They were ideal for defense because they were so dense, soldiers could hide behind them. They were difficult to navigate around, and oftentimes the American troops would run into German soldiers on the other side of the hedge. Tanks could easily plow through the area, but the hedges were set on earth mounds, so getting through the bushes exposed the tanks' underbelly, making it vulnerable to anti-tank weapons. The possibility also existed that the tanks could get tangled in the thick foliage and shed a track, immobilizing it.

The hedgerow country was difficult, but it seemed to Dale that they were taking more fire than anyone. No matter where they went, they were being shot at. He didn't appreciate that very much and tried to figure out what was happening. Then, it became clear. They had a soldier in their group that was fairly tall, and he was carrying his gun propped against his shoulder. The top of it poked above the hedges, alerting the enemy to their position. Once the soldier lowered his weapon, the onslaught of fire minimized.

On one night, while heading through the hedgerow country, Dale heard the faint sounds of tanks. Unsure if they were the Allies or the Germans, he tried not to worry about it because they seemed so far away. In the morning, he woke to find the tanks behind him. Thankfully, they were theirs—General Patton had assembled them to assist—and that made the hedgerow country slightly easier to navigate since the tanks had no problems knocking down the hedges. B17s also bombed the area to clear it of enemy soldiers.

Fighting across France tested Dale's skills and morale. During one battle, they were supposed to take a hill. Battalion headquarters were set up with an aide station, and the soldiers were sent in to fight. As the lines advanced, a quarter of the men were killed every time they tried to take the hill. When Dale was ordered to take his men up, he refused. It was the only time in his career he didn't obey an order. The riflemen also refused. Finally, after an air strike on the hill, they were able to take it.

At nights, the soldiers would settle into their fox holes. One evening, while sitting in his fox hole, Dale had a visitor. Nathan, a soldier barely 18 years old from Indianapolis, jumped in the hole. He said he'd been thinking about Dale.

"I sure don't want your position," the young man said. "All of us really like you and we think you're going to make it. Let's make a pact."

Nathan suggested that if one of them didn't make it but the other did, the survivor would visit the deceased's parents. Dale agreed, but tried to ease Nathan's fears that they were both going to make it home.

The next day, as they moved out, Dale noticed that Nathan wasn't among the group. He headed to the hole Nathan had been in. At some point in the night, a shell had penetrated Nathan's helmet and killed him. Dale collected the young man's personal effects to send home.

A man of his word, Dale had every intention of fulfilling his promise to Nathan to visit his parents when he returned to the states. When the war was finally over, Dale wanted and needed to get back to the ranch. He thought about his promise often and that he needed to get to Indianapolis, but it never worked out. Time slipped by. So much had gone by that Dale felt that Nathan's parents surely had made peace with what had happened to their son, and Dale didn't want to open the wound again. He didn't want to bring up the painful memory. He convinced himself that it was to protect Nathan's parents, but it was also for him. Nathan's death had impacted him deeply, and he didn't want to trudge up harsh memories. To this day, Dale feels like he failed his fellow soldier, and often he wakes up in a cold sweat from nightmares. It was the one and only time Dale had never fulfilled a promise, and he carries the guilt for not sticking to his word.

As Dale and his fellow soldiers made their way through France, the French people were thrilled to have them there. Most of their progress was done on foot, but every so often, the troops were moved by vehicles. On one occasion, Dale and his unit were riding through a part of France known for its hard apple cider, so there were lots of orchards around. The French wanted to give the soldiers gifts, but after being flattened by Germany, the only thing they had left were apples. The French showed up with their aprons full, ready to present these gifts to the Americans. However, since the troops were on the move, they couldn't stop to interact with the French.

Soldier identified as Paul Adams in Dale's war scrapbook (courtesy of the American Heritage Center, ah12622_1_1).

Soldier identified as Stark's friend in Dale's war scrapbook (courtesy of the American Heritage Center, ah12622_1_1).

Dale, July 1945 (courtesy of the American Heritage Center, ah12622_1_1).

"Sgt. Robinson" (courtesy of the American Heritage Center, ah12622_1_1).

Dale and unidentified soldiers (courtesy of the American Heritage Center, ah12622_1_1).

Dale had been riding in the front seat of a jeep and watched the French line the roads. Even though the soldiers were on a mission and couldn't stop, that didn't hinder the French from bestowing their gifts. They would throw the apples at the troops as they passed. This wasn't done with malicious intent; they really wanted the soldiers to know how much they were appreciated. However, the apples were hard and green, and it became apparent which soldiers didn't or couldn't duck when the apples came sailing in. Many men sported black eyes from getting hit or had teeth knocked out.

And so the war went across France. The allies slowly gained land and pushed the Germans back. But the battles weren't easily won. Both sides suffered heavy losses. Dale served as the company leader the vast majority of the time he was in combat, and he saw new replacements show up every night. Sadly, most of them were gone before he even learned their first names. He attributes his survival to digging a hole every time they stopped.

"I dug my way across Europe," he exclaims.

The war in France was tough, but what lay ahead of Dale and the other soldiers promised to test even the sturdiest warrior.

CHAPTER 4:

THE BATTLE OF THE BULGE

There were two moments during WWII that scared Dale to death: crossing the channel into France and the Bulge. As D-Day approached, tensions ran high among the troops. Dale and his fellow soldiers believed they were destined to go in with the first wave.

"I kinda wanted to," said Dale.

After all, that was his objective going into the service.

"I was young and dumb. I wanted to go into combat. I wanted to save our country, you know? I was very patriotic, and I think most of the people was."

Those that weren't, those that wanted an easy was off the battlefield, would resort to shooting themselves in the foot—literally. Dale heard their hollering from across the field. He claimed that he could always tell when the wound was self-inflicted because of the way the soldier screamed.

When Dale was in France, with the exception of the apple incident, they didn't see the French often. They stayed in hiding. But he noticed how beautiful their gardens were. Often, when the men were hungry and craving fresh meat, there was a bounty of chicken and pigs to eat. Being from a ranch, Dale was skilled in performing slaughtering tasks, and the soldiers ate like kings. This type of feast didn't happen often, but the soldiers were thankful when it did. For Dale, it gave a sense of normalcy and a brief reprieve from the true reason why he was there. It didn't change that he had to fight or alleviate fears, but it was a small luxury.

As the war raged on and lives continued to be lost, Dale did what was required to survive. He protected his fellow men with his machine gun and dug foxholes to keep him safe. One can only imagine the death and atrocities he witnessed daily. However bad Dale thought the day-to-day fighting was, it was about to get worse. The Battle of the Bulge became the true test of Dale and his fellow soldiers' courage, stamina, and sanity.

Like D-Day, Hitler wanted to use the element of surprise against the Allies at the Battle of the Bulge.[1] He knew he had to do something drastic to swing the momentum of victory back to his favor. The Allied drive across France had taken its toll on German morale and the number of troops. His plan was to launch a major offensive, using the foggy weather to his advantage. The goal was to send 250,000 men through the Ardennes Forest, which was lightly defended, across the Meuse River and to Antwerp—all in a week. Antwerp was the final destination because it was an Allied supply port.

To accomplish this task, Hitler had to call back thousands of troops from the Russian Front. There, 300 Soviet divisions were preparing to invade Germany. But Hitler was willing to take the risk. He figured it was an opportunity to split apart the powerful American army and crush the British and Canadian holds on the Belgian-Dutch border.[1] He was confident this battle would be over quickly, then he could send his troops back to the Russian Front. He was also convinced that the Allied defeat in this battle would cause the collapse of the Western Alliance.

Hitler's commanding officers didn't have the same confidence. He appointed Field Marshals Model and Rundstedt to lead the offensive, and they knew they had insufficient manpower to pull it off. But voicing their concerns wouldn't sway Hitler. In fact, after the operation had started and the Germans were losing, Hermann Goring, Hitler's oldest comrade, pleaded with him to consider an armistice, and Hitler threatened to have him shot.

The offensive was named Operation Autumn Fog, and like D-Day, it relied on deception to be successful. The Germans created fake radio transmissions that were sent to frontline command posts that didn't exist and false rumors were spread in public spaces. While this was occurring, three whole armies, including 12 Panzer tank divisions, were moved into position.

In addition to deception, Hitler also planned to confuse the Allies. He had created a special school called the "School for Americans" run by SS spy master Otto Skorzeny that trained 2,000 German commandos to speak and act like American soldiers. They had American uniforms and jeeps and were going to create havoc by giving Allied troops coming into the area bad directions, changing road signs, killing dispatch riders, cutting phone wires and attempting to generate panic and hopelessness.[1]

Operation Autumn Fog began at 5:30 a.m. on December 16, 1944. Along an 85-mile long front in the Ardennes, an hour long artillery barrage occurred. There were American divisions defending the area, but they weren't overly effective at stopping the advance. Three of the divisions had no battle experience and the others were battle weary. They were taken by surprise by 2,500 tanks and self-propelled guns, along with 18 infantry divisions.

More often than not, the Germans had the more advanced weapons throughout the war. Their tanks could outmaneuver and outgun anything the Allies had. Their *third-ranking* tank was at least equal to the Allies' *best* tank.[2] The one that struck the most fear was the Tiger, which came in a couple different forms.

The Tiger II, also known as the Tiger B, King Tiger, and Royal Tiger, sported a 600-horsepower engine and a maximum speed of 21 miles per hour. It carried a crew of five and had a cruising range of more than 100 miles.[2] It easily knocked out Allied tanks from a considerable range, and the armor was so thick, there were very few weapons that could destroy it.

There was also the Tiger I, which made its debut in the war in August 1942.[2] This tank carried a crew of five and had a top speed of 23 miles per hour. It had an 88mm L-56 cannon and two 7.92 machine guns mounted on it. Like its counterpart, this tank was also difficult to take out.

Due to the weather, planes could not provide air support, and the American troops were outnumbered three to one. Some retreated, but others stayed to fight. The Germans pushed forward and encountered little resistance for 5 days. They created a 50-mile westward bulge in the line (which is where the Battle of the Bulge title came from), and 7,500 U.S. soldiers surrendered. The German imposters were succeeding in their mission of causing confusion and distrust. Suspicions among the American troops rose, and after interrogating some of the imposters, the information was shared up and down the front line, causing a psychological blow. It was exactly what Hitler wanted to happen. The soldiers were suspicious of one another. But the effect of the Germans posing as Americans only happened on a small part of the line, so it didn't cause the widespread panic Hitler had hoped for. The American troops, knowing that there were imposters out there, if they didn't know a soldier personally, would ask them questions only a true American would know the answer to, such as questions about baseball. Soon, things started to turn around for the American troops.[1]

Reinforcements were sent in by Eisenhower's top aid General Omar Bradley and slowed the German advance. At the front at Bastogne, the 101st Airborne Division worked to hold the city, and when the Germans demanded they surrender, they refused even though they were vastly outnumbered. This act improved morale everywhere.

On December 22, the fog lifted and the Allied planes—hundreds of them—finally took to the skies. They dropped supplies into Bastogne and machine-gunned anything German.

At this point, the Germans were in trouble. They hadn't accomplished any of the tasks they set out to do, which included taking American fuel stops (which they needed for their own supplies) and making it to the Meuse River. In addition, the vast majority of German soldiers on the field were 16 year olds from the Hitler Youth program—and they were undisciplined and reckless, dying by the hundreds.[1]

Hitler's commanders begged him to reconsider his plan, but Hitler refused. Instead, he ordered 25,000 relief troops to the Ardennes. He also ordered a smaller offensive to occur further southward, hoping to draw Allied troops from the north and allow the Germans to continue the drive to the Meuse River. His plan was doomed to fail.

The British had resumed regular radio communications and deciphered the German strategy with the Enigma. The information was relayed to the American troops, who kept up the pressure and drove the Germans back into Germany. Field Marshal Montgomery controlled the American 1st and 9th Armies in the north, and Patton's 3rd Army came up from the south. More than 20,000 Germans failed to escape and were captured on January 16th.

Despite the German's advantage in highly advanced weaponry and tanks, the Tigers were at a disadvantage in the forest. Their weight made it near impossible for them to traverse the soft terrain. They were also short on supplies, especially fuel, and the Tiger II used up a lot. The Tigers were also confined to being on the narrow roads or on solidly frozen ground, otherwise their treads would sink. If they ran out of fuel, they were abandoned, often blocking the path of troops behind them.[2] This issue, in conjunction with all of the other things that went wrong for the Germans, ensured the Allies the victory at the Battle of the Bulge.

What Hitler hoped would be a successful campaign turned out to be costly. The Germans lost 120,000 soldiers and 600 tanks.[1] It was also costly for the Americans. They suffered more than 100,000 casualties, and the Battle of the Bulge had been the most expensive action ever fought.[3]

For Dale and the other soldiers, fighting this battle put all of their skills to the test and pushed them to the brink. Weather conditions were far from ideal. The fog was so thick, it was hard to discern who was friend or foe. All that could be seen were silhouettes. But the battle raged on because the Germans refused to go down without a fight.

With the fog so thick, the Germans would find their targets from the muzzle flash of guns when they fired. Dale was aware of this, but he couldn't stop firing at the enemy. His job was to protect his fellow soldiers. They knew where he was and fired at his location. The bullet caught Dale's friend, a man they called Sarge, in the stomach. Dale was almost out of ammo, so he expended his last rounds, buried his gun and the tripod, and grabbed Sarge. The man was too large to carry, so Dale dragged him out, propped on Dale's back.

"Robi," Sarge said (everyone called Dale "Robi," short for Robinson), "leave me here. I'm going to die."

But Dale wouldn't. He was determined to get Sarge to safety.

Dale had no idea where he was or where he was supposed to go. The fog was so thick he could barely see, and it was snowing. On top of that, the line was constantly changing with the Americans driving forward and being pushed back. All around him Dale heard the Germans speaking their native tongue, and he desperately hoped he didn't run into anyone in the fog.

He walked for what seemed like forever, still unsure if he was heading in the right direction. Sarge kept pleading with him to leave him, but this request fell on deaf ears. Dale trudged on.

"Halt!"

The words hit Dale's ears and relief washed over him. The voice was distinctly American. He'd been heading in the right direction.

"Don't shoot!" Dale said. "I'm American."

After a brief discussion, Sarge was taken from Dale's back to receive medical attention. Dale never saw him again after that. He wrote home to his parents that Sarge had been killed. He was devastated. Sarge had been from Carbine, Kentucky, and often received letters from his wife, but since he couldn't read, Dale read them to him. They were dedicated to one another, brothers in arms, and Dale knew that Sarge would have never left him in the field either.

Thankfully, Dale had been wrong about Sarge's fate, and he was relieved to discover that Sarge didn't die. He was patched up and sent home. After the war, Dale had the intention of visiting Sarge in Kentucky, but never got the chance, and it turned out it worked to his benefit. Dale had the opportunity to meet Sarge's son in 2004, who had been named after Dale, and he informed Dale that where they lived was incredibly rural. If Dale had shown up and asked about Sarge, the locals would have assumed he was a tax collector and probably killed him and thrown him into a ditch—and no one would have known.

Sarge eventually died, and the circumstances were incredibly tragic. According to Sarge's son, his father was shot by a neighbor while milking cows.

After getting Sarge to medical treatment, Dale learned that they were the last two left on the front line. The rest of their platoon had been killed. For his heroism and dedication to a fellow soldier, Dale didn't receive a medal. Rather, he was threatened with a court martial for leaving his weapon in the field.

In addition to the fog, freezing temperatures wreaked havoc on the soldiers. Rarely equipped with the proper winter gear, Dale used his raincoat as a blanket and a tent. As he breathed, his breath condensed and froze, creating solid frost on his coat. On the ground around him would be a thin layer of ice. When he woke in the morning, he would shake off the ice and frost, and the Germans saw the movement and shot. Even though they weren't sure what they were shooting at, it was better not to take chances, and Dale's coat paid the price.

Excerpt from Dale's war scrapbook about Walter Sargent (courtesy of the American Heritage Center, ah12622_1_1).

Smoking also proved difficult during the Bulge. Dale hadn't smoked in a long time, but many of his fellow soldiers did, and any point of light in the fog was a beacon for enemy fire. Even if the soldier was burrowed under his coat, the light was easily seen. For the sake of safety, soldiers didn't smoke at the Bulge.

When German soldiers were captured during the Battle of the Bulge, they were often wearing U.S.-issued equipment, including socks and shoes. It's possible that the German soldiers took the clothes off fallen Americans to combat the extreme weather conditions—both sides were desperate to stay warm and did what was necessary to survive—but it could also be possible that these were some of Hitler's special soldiers trying to infiltrate the lines. Dale doesn't mention anything about this deception, so it's impossible to say for sure.

Photo of Sarge's wife, Alta Mae (courtesy of the American Heritage Center, ah12622_1_1).

Dale never felt hatred toward the Germans during these trying times. He sympathized with them. They were all in the same boat. They were all humans.

During the Bulge, since Dale didn't smoke, he offered a German POW his cigarettes, which happened to be some Raleigh's.

"Nein, nein," came the reply. "Lucky Strike."

Dale laughed. Even the Germans were used to smoking higher quality cigarettes.

It had surprised Dale that Hitler would attempt what he did at the Bulge. The morale of the soldiers was so low. But Hitler was a gambler, and he thought he saw a flaw. Obviously, it didn't work out for him, but it was the only option Hitler had left.

During the Bulge, Dale saw more SS officers than he had during the entire war. SS units were known for their brutality and murderous ways. Originally created to serve as Hitler's personal bodyguards, by the start of WWII, SS numbers had grown to 250,000 members within multiple subdivisions. They engaged in activities ranging from intelligence operations to running the concentration camps.[4]

Becoming an SS member meant that the solider had to prove none of their ancestors were Jewish, and they agreed to marry only with the consent of their superior officers. They were given highly elite training, and they were also taught that they were the elite not only of the Nazi party but of all humankind. They were expected to value allegiance and obligation to the Nazi party above everything else, including individual concerns, and they were to perform their duties as a cohesive unit. They specialized in brutalizing and murdering people in the territories occupied by the Nazis, and they did so effectively and efficiently.

As the war progressed, the SS units increased in numbers, but there are differing accounts as to how many there actually were. Some say there were 800,000, while others report 910,000.[4] In either case, civilians and soldiers alike tried to steer clear of these troops. They were unforgiving and rarely took hostages. But that didn't change the mission, and Dale continued to do his job to ensure the success of the Allies.

Dale was lucky during the Bulge. He had been wounded, taking some shrapnel in the thigh, but he declined going to the medical tent. He knew that men were losing limbs and their lives in there, and he refused to go in with what he perceived to be a minor wound. He had the medic field dress it and continued on with the battle. To this day, he still has fragments in his leg. An MRI revealed calcified objects in his thigh, but since they pose no threat to his life and aren't causing him undue pain, he's never had them removed.

Dale was also lucky that he never got a cold or frost bite, despite the harsh conditions. He attributes this to the shots and vaccines he received from the Army and the fact that when he could, he would light small fires to dry his clothes.

After the Allied victory at the Bulge, Dale and his fellow soldiers were moved to British control, and the war raged on.

Dale and his weapon (courtesy of the American Heritage Center, ah12622_1_1).

Soldier identified as Evel Carnley in Dale's war scrapbook (courtesy of the American Heritage Center, ah12622_1_1).

Unidentified soldiers from Dale's war scrapbook (courtesy of the American Heritage Center, ah12622_1_1).

Unidentified soldiers from Dale's war scrapbook (courtesy of the American Heritage Center, ah12622_1_1).

Soldier identified as Smith in Dale's war scrapbook (courtesy of the American Heritage Center, ah12622_1_1).

Dale and unidentified soldier (courtesy of the American Heritage Center, ah12622_1_1). According to Dale, a captain would get him out of the 60-mile hikes by having him type letters.

Soldier identified as Stark in Dale's war scrapbook (courtesy of the American Heritage Center, ah12622_1_1).

Unidentified soldiers from Dale's war scrapbook (courtesy of the American Heritage Center, ah12622_1_1).

CHAPTER 5:

ACTS OF HEROISM

Dale didn't join the Army to receive medals and become a hero, but that was exactly what happened. He was the recipient of three: the Silver Star, the Bronze Star, and the British Military Medal. He probably could have received more—including a Purple Heart for being wounded in battle—but awards didn't matter to him. All he wanted to do was his job so he could get home and work on the ranch.

Dale received the British Military Medal and the Silver Star for the same event, but he doesn't recall what event that was. Dale was never informed who or when he was reported to a senior officer or what action he did to get these awards. Most soldiers at the time weren't. To him, he was simply doing his job and helping out his fellow soldiers. The official paperwork for the British Military Medal states that he received the award:

> For gallantry in action against the enemy on 23 October 1944, in France. During a strong enemy counter-attack, Sergeant Robinson and his heavy machine gun crew, were in a concealed position, helping to defend friendly territory. Noticing an enemy armored vehicle approaching from the flank, Sergeant Robinson ordered the remainder of the squad to remain in place while he and his gunner (who volunteered) left their concealed position to take up one completely exposed to the enemy. Here they engaged the enemy vehicle in a point-blank

duel and despite the direct cannon fire from the enemy, they succeeded in disabling the enemy car. Remaining in their exposed position, they then commenced firing on enemy troops who were infiltrating toward them behind some enemy tanks, and despite the devastating fire from the tanks, held off a numerically superior force. When the gunner was wounded by enemy fire, Sergeant Robinson immediately took his place and, alone and unaided, continued to deliver devastating fire on the enemy. When a group of the enemy infiltrated to within hand grenade range of their position, Sergeant Robinson and the wounded gunner proceeded to neutralize them with pistol fire. The inspirational courage, fearless determination, and tenacity of purpose displayed by the gallant actions of Sergeant Robinson reflects highest credit on himself and the armed forces of the Allied Nations. (see Figure 5.1)

The citation for his Silver Star reads slightly different. It says:

Corporal Lance D. Robinson, 37357605, 313th Infantry, United States Army, for gallantry in action against the enemy on 23 October 1944, in France. During a strong enemy counterattack, Corporal Robinson helped his gunner displace a machine gun from a concealed position to a completely exposed position in order to fire on an enemy armored vehicle. They engaged the enemy vehicle in a point blank duel and in spite of direct cannon fire from the enemy succeeded in disabling the car. They then commenced firing on enemy troops who were infiltrating behind tanks and despite fire from the tanks, held off a numerically superior force. When the gunner was wounded Corporal Robinson immediately took his place and, unaided, continued to deliver devastating fire on the enemy. When a group of the enemy infiltrated to within hand grenade range of their position, Corporal Robinson and the wounded gunner proceeded to neutralize them with pistol fire. The inspirational courage, zealous determination and tenacity displayed by Corporal Robinson reflect highest credit on himself and the armed forces of the United States. (see Figure 5.2)

Figure 5.1 Copy of Dale's British Military Medal citation.

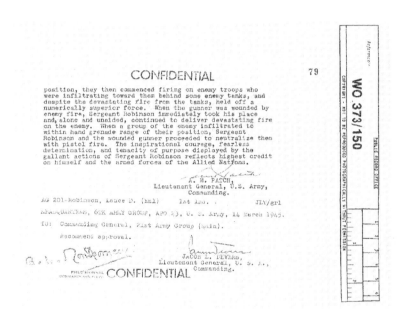

Figure 5.1 Copy of Dale's British Military Medal citation (continued).

R E S T R I C T E D

HEADQUARTERS 79TH INFANTRY DIVISION
APO 79, U. S. Army

GENERAL ORDERS)   16 December 1944

NUMBER.....109)

        I. Posthumous Award of Silver Star.
        II. Award of Silver Star.

        I. POSTHUMOUS AWARD OF SILVER STAR. Pursuant to authority contained
in AR 600-45, The Silver Star is awarded posthumously to the following named
officer and enlisted men.

        First Lieutenant LAWRENCE H. THOMAS, 01285334, Infantry, 315th Infan-
try, United States Army, for gallantry in action against the enemy on 22 October
1944, in France. While voluntarily engaged in a reconnaissance mission to improve the field of fire of his platoon which was resisting an enemy counterattack, Lieutenant THOMAS crawled to within thirty five yards of an enemy machine
gun emplacement and attacked the position with a rifle. His intrepid action
caused the surrender of six enemy soldiers and one officer. Other enemy soldiers
then fled in disorder and were brought down by fire from the platoon. The entire
action was accomplished at great personal risk and under intense enemy fire from
machine guns and mortars. The dauntless courage and fidelity to duty displayed
by Lieutenant THOMAS reflect highest credit on himself and the armed forces of
the United States.

        Technical Sergeant Michael F. Spinn, 35309326, 313th Infantry, United
States Army, for gallantry in action against the enemy on 5 August 1944, in
France. When an enemy machine gun, which was so well concealed in a hedgerow
that riflemen were unable to locate it and the mortar observer was hampered like-
wise, Technical Sergeant Spinn, voluntarily crawled forward under intense fire
and neutralized the position with hand grenades. His heroic action regained contact with units which had become separated by the intensity of the fire from the
enemy emplacement and permitted the advance to resume. The dauntless courage
and devotion to duty, without regard for his own safety, reflect highest credit
on Technical Sergeant Spinn and the armed forces of the United States.

        Staff Sergeant Eugene Lucas, 34475178, 314th Infantry, United States
Army, for gallantry in action against the enemy on 22 September 1944, in France.
Staff Sergeant Lucas, without regard for his own personal safety, voluntarily
left the cover of a deep ditch and ran into an open field to fire at enemy artillery positions with a rifle grenade in order to indicate the location of the
enemy positions to a supporting unit attacking through woods. When the first
grenade failed to explode he returned to the ditch, procured another, and repeated the hazardous process. This attempt succeeded and the supporting unit was
able to bring intense fire upon the enemy. Under cover of this fire, Staff Sergeant Lucas led his squad in a frontal assault on the enemy strongpoint, and it
was while thus gallantly engaged that he fell, mortally wounded. The dauntless
courage, aggressive leadership and fidelity to duty displayed by Staff Sergeant

                                        - 1 -

                            R E S T R I C T E D

Figure 5.2 Copy of Dale's Silver Start Citation.

R E S T R I C T E D

(GO 109, Hq 79th Inf Div, 16 Dec 44, contd)

rocket launcher, and took up a position commanding the trail being used by the tank. Holding his fire until the tank was within ten yards of his position, he scored a direct hit on the turret with his first round, killing the occupants of the turret and forcing the tank to withdraw. The courage and initiative displayed by Sergeant Miller reflect highest credit on himself and the armed forces of the United States.

Sergeant Joe J. Maas, 6248897, 315th Infantry, United States Army, for gallantry in action against the enemy on 23 October 1944, in France. When his squad became confused before a direct assault by an enemy tank supported by infantry, and intense machine gun fire from the tank forced the men to take cover, Sergeant Maas, sensing the urgency of the situation, instantly rallied the squad and brought the fire of all small arms and a light machine gun to bear on the enemy infantrymen. He directed his squad so ably that the enemy riflemen withdrew in confusion, and the tank, left without infantry support, followed suit. Sergeant Maas' outstanding leadership and gallantry reflect highest credit on himself and the armed forces of the United States.

Corporal Dale D. Robinson, 3735'806, 315th Infantry, United States Army, for gallantry in action against the enemy on 23 October 1944, in France. During a strong enemy counterattack, Corporal Robinson helped his gunner displace a machine gun from a concealed position to a completely exposed position in order to fire on an enemy armored vehicle. They engaged the enemy vehicle in a point blank duel and in spite of direct cannon fire from the enemy succeeded in disabling the car. They then commenced firing on enemy troops who were infiltrating behind tanks and despite fire from the tanks, held off a numerically superior force. When the gunner was wounded Corporal Robinson immediately took his place and, unaided, continued to deliver devastating fire on the enemy. When a group of the enemy infiltrated to within hand grenade range of their position, Corporal Robinson and the wounded gunner proceeded to neutralize them with pistol fire. The inspirational courage, zealous determination and tenacity displayed by Corporal Robinson reflect highest credit on himself and the armed forces of the United States.

Private First Class Thomas K. Freeman, 35453594, 314th Infantry, United States Army, for gallantry in action against the enemy on 8 July 1944, in France. When grazing enemy machine gun and intense mortar fire arrested the advance of his platoon and the slightest move brought increased fire to bear, Private First Class Freeman set up a light machine gun under direct enemy observation, and opened fire, thus enabling the platoon to advance to the security of a nearby wall. Though wounded by shell fragments and machine gun fire, he continued to engage the enemy until the entire platoon had advanced to safety. The gallantry and heroic devotion to duty displayed by Private First Class Freeman reflect highest credit on himself and the armed forces of the United States.

- 4 -

R E S T R I C T E D

Figure 5.2 Copy of Dale's Silver Star Citation (continued).

What Dale does recall about the presentation ceremony was that he was on R&R and was told to report to headquarters wearing his Class A uniform. The first thought that ran through his mind was that he was finally going to be court martialed. The incident from the Bulge, when he saved Sarge's life but left his weapon in the field, ran through his mind. He was convinced they were going to make good on their threat.

A jeep came to pick him up, and Dale asked where they were going and why, but the driver couldn't tell him why. He just had orders to take Dale to a specific location. That didn't ease Dale's fears. He was dropped off in front of a building and told to go inside and wait. At this point, he was frantic. What was he going to tell his mom and dad? He was trying to behave in a way that would make them proud, but a court martial would surely disappoint them.

Finally, he was called. Before him were 11 other soldiers lined up at attention. He was ushered to the front of the line. At that moment, he realized he wasn't being court martialed but was receiving a medal, and relief flooded through him. Out of the other soldiers with him, he received the highest honor. Three British generals and two U.S. generals presented him the British Military Medal. Field Marshal Montgomery was one of those generals.

Field Marshal Bernard Montgomery was born in 1887.[1] He served in WWI on the Western Front. A highly efficient young officer, he was given a succession of command posts in Britain and India. By 1938, he had been promoted to major-general.

When WWII broke out, he had been part of the British Expeditionary Force that withstood the Wehrmacht's Blitzkreig. He was given command of the Third Division, which had been evacuated at Dunkirk. He was then given command of the Eighth Army in North Africa after Winston Churchill's sacking of Auchinleck after the failure at El Alamein.

Montgomery's lifestyle wasn't typical of a general. His command base was a large and luxurious house, but he lived in a caravan in the garden. He was anti-smoking, but always made sure his men had access to cigarettes, and he went out of his way to meet the soldiers under his command.

During D-Day, Montgomery commanded the British and Canadian unit tasked with fighting the main bulk of the German forces at Normandy. This allowed the American 12th Army Group to move deeply into France. Montgomery worked with Eisenhower, and they had a professional relationship, but he didn't always agree with Eisenhower's strategy. Montgomery believed that Eisenhower too frequently favored the American plans and the maverick General George Patton.[1]

On September 1, 1944, Montgomery was promoted to Field Marshall, which was the highest rank he could get in the British Army. He had command of the 21st Army Group and took Antwerp in Belgium. This group was also involved with the Battle of the Bulge, and they crossed the Rhine River on March 24, 1945. He accepted the formal surrender of the Germans at Luneburg Heath on May 4, 1945.

After the war, from 1946 to 1948, Montgomery served as Chief of the Imperial General Staff. From 1951 to 1958, he was Deputy Supreme Commander of NATO forces in Europe.

The British Military Medal is the highest medal a soldier outside of the British Army can receive. It was an honor to have it presented by Field Marshall Montgomery. Every one of the generals was proud of what Dale had done and congratulated him on going above and beyond his duty. Dale was mostly happy that he hadn't gotten into trouble and his parents would still be proud of him.

After the ceremony, he climbed back in the jeep and asked where they were headed next. The driver said he was at Dale's whim for the rest of the day, so Dale got to decide. On the way to the award ceremony, they had passed by an ammo dump, and a large pile of guns had caught Dale's eye. He asked the driver to head there.

As he walked around, he realized that there were 2-3 piles of Mauser action rifles piled 6 feet high. The vast majority of them looked to be brand new and never fired. As Dale checked out the pile, the dump guard showed up and asked what they were doing. Dale pointed at the pile of rifles.

"I'd really like a couple of these guns. They'd make great deer rifles," Dale explained.

The guard told him that no one was allowed to take the guns, so Dale explained that he'd just won an award and showed the guard the medal.

"You know," the guard said. "I like you. I have to go to the other end." And he turned his back on Dale and the driver.

Dale took that as a sign and grabbed two rifles before loading back into the jeep.

When Dale returned home, he took the guns to a local gunsmith, who had never seen a Mauser action. One of the guns had a .22 insert inside the barrel, and Dale had him take it out so it could take regular ammo. The gunsmith carved a deer jumping over a log away from a hunter into the stock. The gun currently belongs to Dale's daughter Ade and has been used on several hunting trips.

Dale was also awarded the Bronze Star for performing his job in a heroic manner. The official paperwork reads:

> Sergeant Lance D. Robinson, 37357605, Infantry, 313th Infantry, United States Army, for meritorious achievement in action against the enemy from 19 June 1944 to 15 April 1945, in France, Belgium, the Netherlands, and Germany. Throughout this extended period of combat Sergeant Robinson performed his duties as squad leader in a most capable and efficient manner. Exhibiting unusual ingenuity and sound judgement in his execution of assigned functions he contributed greatly to the effective combat operations of his unit. The initiative and devotion to duty displayed by Sergeant Robinson reflect great credit on the armed

forces of the United States. Entered military service from (not available). (see Figure 5.3)

All of his medals are on display in a shadow box that hangs in his home. They are both a reminder of his heroic deeds and what he did for his country and a time of great sadness and loss.

In addition to these heroic deeds that Dale received recognition for, he also carried out actions that didn't get him any awards. Saving Sarge's life was one. Another was saving the lives of many during one particular campaign.

Dale was color blind, which kept him out of the Army Air Corps (the military branch he really wanted to join) and almost disqualified him from being in the Army. However, it was this "disability" that helped him and his fellow soldiers. During the campaign, the troops were getting ready to make a drive, but Dale could see that their intended path would lead them into danger. He turned to the commander.

"You need to knock out that tank with a bazooka first," Dale told him.

If they didn't, the cannon was aimed right down the middle of the troops and would cause untold devastation and loss of life.

Sergeant Lance D. Robinson, 37357506, Infantry, 313th Infantry, United States Army, for meritorious achievement in action against the enemy from 19 June 1944 to 15 April 1945, in France, Belgium, the Netherlands, and Germany. Throughout this extended period of combat Sergeant Robinson performed his duties as squad leader in a most capable and efficient manner. Exhibiting unusual ingenuity and sound judgment in his execution of assigned functions he contributed greatly to the effective combat operations of his unit. The initiative and devotion to duty displayed by Sergeant Robinson reflect great credit on the armed forces of the United States. Entered military service from (not available).

Figure 5.3 Copy of Dale's Bronze Star Citation.

The commander had no idea what Dale was talking about. He couldn't see the tank, so he was sure there was no threat and commanded the troops forward. But Dale insisted it was there. Confusion ensued. Dale was adamant that scouts should be sent out—it would save lives. Eventually, the commander reported the findings to a higher ranking officer and scouts were sent out. The tank was discovered in the bushes and knocked out. From there, the drive proceeded forward.

In another campaign, he and his fellow soldiers were responsible for freeing American POWs in Hammelburg. Unfortunately, Dale doesn't remember this particular event in detail, only recalls that they met little resistance from the Germans and that the soldiers were incredibly happy to see them.

The Hammelburg Raid[2] was a secret and controversial operation that took place 80 km behind enemy lines by the 4th U.S. Armored Division on March 26-28, 1945. General Patton personally ordered the attack, and it was commanded by Captain Abraham J. Baum. The goal was to liberate U.S. POWs at camp OFLAG XIII-B, which was near Hammelburg. Officially, it was a rescue mission. Secretly, it was to rescue Patton's son-in-law, LTC John K. Waters, who had been captured in 1945 at the Kasserine Pass in Tunisia.

Founded in 1895 as a training installation for the Royal Bavarian Army, Camp Hammelburg was transformed into a POW camp during WWI. In 1935, it became a training camp again, then parts were used again as a POW camp in WWII.

OFLAG XIII-B was a POW camp for officers. The first occupants were Serbian officers, but after the Battle of the Bulge, the camp was split into two compounds: one for Serbian officers and the other for American officers. POWs were contained in solid stone buildings, and it was estimated that 3,000 Serbian and 1,500 Americans were kept there.

The attack on the compound was incredibly difficult. Baum lost 30% of the men and vehicles involved before finally reaching their destination. In total, 26 out of the 314 officers and men were killed and 57 vehicles were destroyed or captured by the Germans.[2] Once they made it into the camp, it became evident that there were too many prisoners for Captain Baum to take back. They were told to expect 300, but there were far more. Tired and weary, Baum and his men rested at the camp, and during the night, the Germans took the opportunity to surround it. Captain Baum and his men became POWs themselves. The raid had failed.

However, 10 days later on April 5, 1945, the 14th U.S. Armored Division liberated the camp.[2] When Dale and his fellows soldiers came into play for this battle is unknown. However, all of the surviving POWs were rescued.

In addition to some of the specific battles, Dale recalls that airplanes were a constant sight during the war—both Allied and enemy. On more than one occasion, planes would decide the outcome of a battle. Dale and his fellow soldiers spent many occasions being pinned down by air fire while trekking across France, and they also called in their own planes to gun down the Germans. At night, planes would do flyovers and recon missions. There was one particular plane that was well known to Dale and his men. It flew over almost every night, and was recognizable by a distinctive *baloom, baloom, baloom* noise that it made. It was a German recon plane, and Dale and his men nicknamed it Bed Check Charlie because it almost always flew over while they were settling down for the night.

The war to destroy Hitler's tyranny was hard won, but with grit and determination, the Allied forces accomplished the task. The loss of lives was staggering, but Dale was one of the fortunate ones to have survived.

After the Germans surrendered, Dale was sent to Czechoslovakia. One of the things that amazed Dale about his stay here was how the women would take their baskets into the mountains and cut grass with a scythe. The slopes were steep, but the women seemed to have no issues traversing the terrain. They would slice the grass short, reminding Dale of the well-manicured lawns in the U.S., then stack it into super high piles in baskets. After bringing the load down the steep slopes, the grass was then placed in the front yards as hay for the milk cows.

He was also impressed with how good of cooks the Czechs were, and surprised at the amount of vodka they drank. He and two other soldiers were staying with the mayor of the town, and every morning before they went to breakfast, the mayor would meet them at the door with glasses of vodka. Dale and the other soldiers tried various ways to get out of the house without having to take a drink, but they usually failed. The mayor always found them. Not wanting to be rude or offensive—the mayor was simply trying to express his gratitude to them for being there—they would grab their glasses and throw the clear liquid back. Instantly, the vodka would take their breath away because it was so potent. They would head out onto the streets, smacking each other on the backs so that they could once again catch their breath. The mayor never let the vodka in the decanter get below the neck, and he never let Dale and his friends leave without taking a drink.

Life in Czechoslovakia was pretty laid back. There weren't any enemy soldiers they had to worry about, and no one was trying to kill them. But there were still a few issues that needed to be taken care of, and one of those was Russian soldiers stealing the locals' cows.

Dale hadn't had any contact with Russian soldiers during combat, but after, he was asked to deter them from taking livestock. The Russian soldiers seemed to always know when the people in the town butchered animals, and they came at night to steal them. The mayor was tired of it, so he asked Dale and the soldiers to set up in an attic and take care of the problem. He told Dale that it would be all right if they killed the Russians—after all, they were committing a crime—but Dale felt that was a bit severe. The mayor set up a beef in the yard below the window, and when the Russians showed up that night in their pickup, Dale and his friends shot over their heads from their position in the attic. They didn't kill anyone, and that was enough to deter them. The rest of the time Dale and the U.S. soldiers were there, the Russians didn't come back to steal any meat.

While in Czechoslovakia, there were rumors that Dale and his unit might have to go to the South Pacific for 3 months. This didn't sit well with Dale, but there wasn't much he could do about the situation. He would go where they told him to go and do his job to the best of his abilities. Because of this, the troops were expected to continue doing drills, which made many of them unhappy. The landscape wasn't exactly conducive to marching, and they often had to do it on the sides of steep hills. Dale felt that the drills were ridiculous, especially since they were seasoned veterans, so he protested as much as he could without getting into too much trouble. One tactic he and a few others used was to attach blocks to the bottom of their feet so that they could walk normal on the steep inclines.

A month passed in Czechoslovakia before the men were informed of their next destination. Much to Dale's relief, he wasn't sent to the South Pacific. After 3 years in the Army, at almost 21 years of age, Dale was going home.

CHAPTER 6:

COMING HOME

When Dale disembarked the ship after it had landed in the U.S., the first thing he saw were coolers lining the path that were stuffed full of milk. The white liquid was a luxury they weren't afforded overseas, and Dale took the opportunity to drink his fill.

Dale's time in the war was done. The experience had been bittersweet. Many young men's lives had been lost in the conflict; many of whom Dale didn't know. But there had also been those whom he had known extremely well. He had one friend that he'd been close with since they first got overseas. The two of them made it through the worst of the battles. While taking a break one day from the march, Dale's friend took a seat next to a crumbled building wall. At about that same time, a convoy of tanks was passing on the streets, and the vibrations shook the rest of the wall loose, burying his friend in rubble and killing him.

There were a few moments when Dale and his fellow soldiers had a reprieve from the death and destruction, and those came in the form of USO shows. Dale and his fellow men would walk for miles to see these shows, and sat on the ground to watch. He was able to see Bob Hope, Bing Crosby, Sammy Davis, Jr., Dean Barton, and Jackie Gleeson.

On one R&R trip, right before he left for home, Dale spent some time with his brother in England. He visited his brother on the naval base, and met his brother's wife and her family. They weren't particularly nice to him, so he decided to stay with a girl he'd met. Her family was incredibly kind to him, and she had her sights set on the U.S., but Dale left her hanging.

These moments of reprieve were few and far between and never lasted long enough, but Dale was thankful for them.

When he returned home, he expected things would return to the way they had been before he'd left, but they didn't. Things had changed. Dale had changed. He had been forced to grow up while overseas, and he was no longer a boy working on the ranch. He had dreams of owning his own ranch and planned on using the money he'd sent home from the war to buy it.

While in the kitchen with his father, news came that the ranch adjacent to theirs was for sale. He told his dad they should buy it. It would be a great investment and expand their operation. His father thought that was a great idea, but what money would they use?

"My pay checks that I sent home when I was overseas," answered Dale.

His father became confused. "We didn't get any pay checks."

And then Dale realized that *none* of the money he'd made while doing his patriotic duty had made it home. His 18 months in combat was for nothing.

But that wasn't the last of his issues. In addition to having his wages stolen, Dale was also suffering from physical ailments. As a heavy machine gunner, the requirements of his job were to carry his weapon everywhere he went. At that time, he thought nothing of it because it was his job. But when he returned home and tried to perform his duties on the ranch, it became apparent the war had taken its toll. Some mornings, he wasn't able to lift his arms above his head. His dad or his wife had to help him saddle and bridle his horse, otherwise he wouldn't be able to get his work done for the day. He was in constant pain. His back always hurt.

Dale's brother, Herb (courtesy of the American Heritage Center, ah12622_1_1).

His uncle worked out of McFadden as an oil worker, and they had a company doctor for the Marathon Oil workers. This doctor had lost his wife, so his daughter moved in with him, and Dale's wife's sister became really good friends with her. They talked about how bad Dale's shoulders were, so the doctor told him to come see him.

They lived about 4 or 5 miles outside of town and were busy so didn't make it in often. However, one day they were driving through town and happened to see the doctor on the street. Dale pulled over and introduced himself.

"Well, I've been wondering when you were going to come in," said the doctor. "What's a matter with ya?"

Dale explained, "I can't raise my arms above my head. It's arthritis or rheumatism or something."

"How did ya get that?"

Dale explained how when he was in the service he had to sleep in fox holes covered in ice.

"Well, that's a pretty good explanation," admitted the doctor.

He then reached into his pocket and pulled out a bunch of pills. Sorting through them, he handed Dale six to eight pills and told him to take them until they were gone. They worked like magic! They helped Dale so much, he went back and got more, but then the doctor died.

He knew he couldn't live without the pills, so his sister-in-law went to the doctor's daughter and asked if they could get more pills. The daughter explained that she could order all his pills, but Dale would have to take an entire jar of them. Dale was fine with that. He had to have them, so she ordered them. When it arrived, it was a square jar with about 5,000 pills in it. They all laughed about the size and put the jar in the closet, but Dale took them whenever his pain got real bad, especially during cold weather, and he got to the point where he could raise his arms over his head.

This certainly wasn't the only time Dale had to deal with injury and pain. While working on the ranch, he took a spill on one of his horses and hurt his shoulder and broke his collar bone. He was in a cast for about 6 weeks, and that made working livestock difficult.

Another time he, a friend, and their fathers were heading to Jackson Hole to do some elk hunting. The area they were going to be in was an 18-mile horse ride into the deep forest. He was riding a mare that he'd been on before and was usually very sure footed. For some reason on this particular trip, she stumbled and went down and Dale went with her. He was able to step right off the saddle and onto the ground.

Drawing of Dale created by fellow soldier (courtesy of the
American Heritage Center, ah12622_1_1). Dale commented on
here that the only thing wrong with the picture is that he didn't
smoke, so he would not have had a cigarette in his mouth.

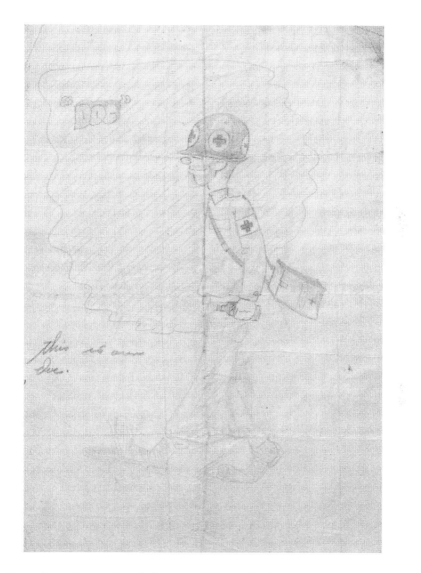

Drawing done by fellow soldier of the company medic (courtesy of the American Heritage Center, ah12622_1_1).

Drawing done by Dale's fellow soldier (courtesy of the American Heritage Center, ah12622_1_1).

He knew immediately that something had gone wrong and took a seat on a log. The horse's saddle horn got caught on the underbrush, and she couldn't get up.

"You've got to get that mare up," his friend said. "Or she's going to die."

"I can't," Dale explained. "I broke my leg."

"How did you break your leg? You stepped off her just as smooth as anything."

Dale nodded. "I know. I don't know what I did, but it's broken."

The friend untangled the saddle horn from the bushes and got the horse onto her feet. He then went over to check on Dale.

Dale had on a pair of tall lace up boots, so his friend set to work getting them off. As soon as they were undone, the bottom half of his leg fell at a 90-degree angle, scaring the hell out both men.

"We've got to get you to a doctor."

Dale wasn't going to argue, but they were a long way from help, and they had to go to camp to let their fathers know what was going on. Using fallen sticks, Dale's friend fashioned a splint and tightened it around Dale's leg. They got back on their horses and headed into camp, where they collected their fathers and headed out.

Dale's father was the excitable type when it came to injuries like this. When they got to the hospital in Jackson Hole, the doctor was unhappy about having to treat Dale. Like Dale's friend, the doctor didn't believe that he had actually broken his leg. He removed the makeshift splints, and once again, Dale's leg fell at a 90-degree angle. Lance was already worked up, so he got into the doctor's face and let him know how much he didn't appreciate the way he was treating his son. The doctor placed Dale in a full-leg cast, which he had to wear for 9 months. When it came time to remove it, he had to go to a doctor in Denver.

That entire time, Dale was unable to work on the ranch, but Jayne picked up most of the slack. Even though Dale was no stranger to injury, breaking his collar bone and his leg didn't have any long-lasting effects. However, the injury to his back he received while in the Army has stuck with him his entire life.

Dale never had a discharge physical when he left the Army, and he lived a long ways from the nearest VA hospital. Living rurally, the only vehicle he had was used on the ranch, and since it wasn't reliable, it wasn't used often. He didn't think he had any recourse from his pain—and he assumed that others were probably going through it was well—so he did nothing about it.

Later in life, Dale endured three different intensive back surgeries, all of which still have yet to relieve the pain. He walks hunched over with a walker, unable to straighten to his full height.

Like many soldiers who came back from combat, Dale suffers from Post-traumatic Stress Disorder (PTSD). Late in his life, he attempted to see several different professionals for his condition, but to no avail. He often left the appointments feeling worse than when he went in. It wasn't until he met Dr. Davis in Phoenix at the medical center that he was able to open up and really talk about his experiences in the war.

But Dale has never been controlled by defeat. Despite the pain and the loss of his wages, he was determined to fulfil his dream. He was going to own his own ranch. Now that the war was out of the way and his life lay before him, Dale got to work. There was just one last thing he had to do to make his Army career final. He had to go back to Denver for his official discharge.

Dale and several thousand other men were taken to the Air Force base in Denver and seated in an auditorium. Career officers gave speeches about how proud they were of the men and the sacrifice they made for their country. They explained that if everyone signed up for the reserves, they would be sent back home. The men couldn't get in line fast enough.

"It was like a stampede," recalls Dale.

But not everyone wanted to sign up. Dale and a few other men remained in their seats. Dale didn't want to be in the reserves. He had done his duty, put in his time, and he wanted to be done with the Army.

They sat there all day waiting for what would happen next. Dale and the others would not relent, and they were willing to do whatever it took to be done with their service. Finally, the officers handed them train tickets and told them to go. Dale and the others received a free ride home *and* they were free from all future obligations to the Army.

Dale married shortly after returning home on May 24, 1945. He had known his bride since he was a kid—their family ranches were adjacent to each other and she was family through marriage. When they were kids, Dale used to take horses to her ranch and pick her up for an all-day ride.

Jayne had moved to Hawaii for her last 2 years of high school, but was back visiting the family. She and Dale hooked up, and before she headed back to Hawaii, she and Dale talked of marriage.

"Why don't we get married?" Jayne asked.

"Honey," explained Dale. "You can do what I do, and I'm gonna ranch the rest of my life." But he felt in his heart that she really didn't want to ranch, which was why she and her family left to go to Hawaii.

"I wanna ranch too."

"I don't think you do."

But Jayne was persistent.

Dale finally relented. "Okay. We're gonna get married, but I'm tellin' ya, you're not gonna like it."

Jayne worked hard on the ranch, putting in 8-hour days and preparing meals and taking care of the kids. She was Dale's best ranch hand, and he couldn't run the ranch without her.

Dale's honorable discharge paper.

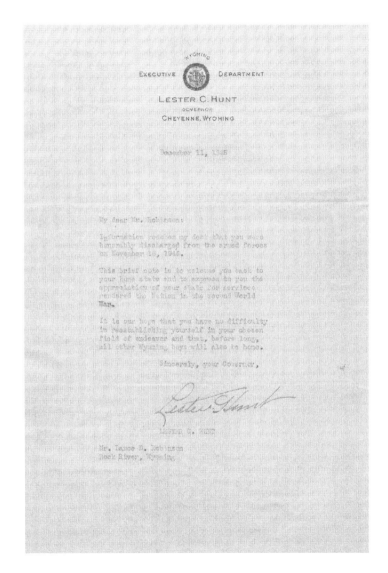

Letter from Lester C. Hunt, former governor of Wyoming, about Dale's honorable discharge from the Army (courtesy of the American Heritage Center, ah12622_1_1).

As a welder and handyman, Dale often tried to create things that would make Jayne's life and work easier. One of these things was a floor buffer. Their ranch house had hardwood floors, and Jayne made sure they always looked immaculate. She would place the wax on the floor and then get down on her hands and knees to buff it with a towel.

One day while welding, Dale's attention was drawn to an 18-inch cylinder that had been cut out of 1/4-inch plate. He had a 1-horse-power drill with handles on each side that only weighed 35-40 pounds, so he figured that would make a great buffer. The only issue he could foresee was that the trigger on the drill wasn't working right, so he had to wire it straight over. That meant that whenever it was plugged in, it would start running. Dale figured that as long as they were aware that was the case, it would be fine. He went to the house and asked Jayne for some old towels, which she was happy to supply, then Dale went back and got to work.

He padded the disk with all the towels, then using curved needles he used for veterinary procedures on the cows, he sewed the towels at the edges to make a soft buffer. After measuring the disk 25 different ways, he found dead center and welded a 5/8-inch bolt to the plate. He affixed it to the drill and brought it to the house, where Jayne had just finished putting the wax on the floor.

"I'll help ya," Dale told her as he walked into the house.

"What are you going to do?" Jayne wondered.

"I'm going to buff the floor for ya."

"How are you going to do that?"

Dale smiled. "Just wait and watch." He handed Jayne the end of the cord and said, "Now, when I'm ready, plug this in. But don't do it until I tell you because I don't have any way to stop it."

Dale was convinced the buffer was going to run smoothly. He had a grip on each of the handles of the drill, which came to his mid-thighs, and readied himself.

"Plug it in."

Jayne did as she was told.

Reeeooooor! The buffer bounced off the floor into midair. It came back down to the floor again, and reeeooooor! It took him around the house.

"Shut her off! Shut her off!" Dale yelled. He was convinced the buffer was going to take him through the side of the house.

Jayne struggled to unplug the buffer because she was laughing. Finally, she got the machine unplugged, but not before she wet her pants from laughing so hard.

What Dale hadn't realized before placing the buffer on the floor was that the weld had warped the plate. It wouldn't sit flat. He took the buffer and threw it back into the iron pile. Years later when they moved off the ranch, it was one of the last things he saw.

Dale and Jayne started their own family while living on the ranch and had three children, Lance, Lloyd, and Ade, in addition to an adopted child—not through the courts, legally, but he was loved and raised as one of their own. As they grew, they helped their parents take care of the livestock and kept the ranch running smoothly. Life was always busy on the ranch and everyone had to pull their weight to make sure the work was done. It wasn't always easy, but it was what Dale loved to do.

CHAPTER 7:

LIFE ON THE RANCH

"Daylight never caught me in bed," says Dale when asked what a typical day on the ranch was like.

Often up before the sun to check on the cattle, he went to bed long after the sun was down. Evenings were spent repairing equipment so that work could continue the next day.

When Dale first returned from the war, he went to work for his father. The ranch was a dairy operation, and they supplied milk for Rock River and Laramie. They started out with 12 cows, and as time went on, they acquired between 25 and 30 cows to milk.

Like McFadden, Rock River was established when companies came looking for oil. According to *Wyoming Tales and Trails*, the town was founded as follows:

> In 1917, the Ohio Oil Company which had earlier explored for oil at Grass Creek, Ten Sleep, and in the Lance Creek area turned its attention to an area about 12 1/2 miles south-west of Rock River on the British-owned Cooper Ranch. There, in conjunction with the Continental Oil Company, in May 1918 the first well came in. Suddenly, prosperity came to Rock River. At the site of the well field, a new oil camp originally called "Ohio City" arose. In 1920, the oil camp was renamed McFadden after the Rocky Mountain field superintendent for the Ohio Oil Co, John "Uncle Jack"

McFadyen. In Rock River, the two-story Lincoln Hotel was constructed. The hotel building is still in existence as a private residence. The Bishop Land Company laid out a plan for a commercial district. The town had three banks, the Citizens' State Bank of Rock River, the Rock River State Bank, and the First National Bank of Rock River. An insignia for the town's success was the First National constructed in 1919 and housed in a building that looked like a Greek temple with Ionic columns and Doric pilasters. The town was governed by leading businessmen. The treasurer, H. A. Thompson, was the chief shareholder in the Rock River Mercantile. He was also the chief stockholder in the First National Bank. The town's mayor, Lewis C. Bishop, was the cashier of the Rock River State Bank and later the vice-president of the First National Bank. The town floated through the mayor's bank a bond issue to acquire a water system. All looked rosy for the town's future.[1]

The future didn't end up being rosy for the town, however, and the banks failed due to shady businessmen and questionable business practices. However, Rock River was on the Lincoln Highway route, it was part of the railroad, and it had a thriving ranching industry, so it survived. According to the 2010 census, 245 people called Rock River their home.[2]

Laramie, Wyoming, came into being when the Union Pacific railway came through the state. It started as an "end of the tracks" town, and for a while, lawlessness and vigilantes ran the small town. It wasn't until the fall of 1868, after a few hangings, that the outlaws were driven out of town and things settled down a bit.[3] A year after that, Laramie had a school, churches, stores, and permanent residents. While the railroad was responsible for founding the city, the surrounding area proved to be excellent for cattle and sheep ranching, and those industries contributed to the income of the city. It wasn't long before Laramie had rolling mills for railroad rails, a railroad tie treatment plant, a brick yard, a slaughter house, a brewery, a glass blowing plant, a plaster mill, and many other industries.[3] In 1886, Laramie was one of the first small towns west of the Mississippi to have an electric plant.[3]

Laramie also boasted several other firsts, including the first woman voter to vote in a general election. Mrs. Louisa Gardner Swain was 70 years old when she voted in the September 6, 1870, elections. Laramie also had the first jury that allowed women to serve in March 1870.[3]

In 1886, before Wyoming was even a state, legislation was signed to allow for the establishment of the University of Wyoming, which is still the state's only 4-year university. The first two graduates received their degrees from the University of Wyoming on July 10, 1890.[3]

The railroad and cattle industry were responsible for the growth of Laramie until the 1950s. Then, the Union Pacific switched its steam locomotives to diesel engines and less maintenance was needed. Several shops closed, but Laramie continued to thrive thanks to the ranching industry and the university.

The driving distance from Dale's ranch in McFadden to Laramie was approximately 48 miles, and the driving distance from McFadden to Rock River was approximately 13 miles. Dale and his father delivered milk to Rock River using a horse and wagon. They would tie the team up behind the bar, then head inside to play Pitch, a card game. They would sit there all day, playing for frozen turkeys and hams. Their wives would get so angry at them for "messing around in town," but were happy to get the meat. Dale and Lance won so many turkeys and hams in their games that they didn't have room for them in their freezers.

Dale's goal after returning from overseas was to fulfill his dream. He hadn't given up on wanting his own ranch, and he wasn't going to let a few obstacles stand in his way. Sure, someone in the Army stole all his money, but he could make more. He had a work ethic and job skills, he could manage a ranch and earn enough money to buy his own in the future. There were plenty of ranches and opportunities in the vicinity for him to make it on his own.

Dale was determined to make it, so he started applying for jobs in the area. Ranch after ranch rejected him, telling him that he was too young. He was frustrated by the responses, but Dale wasn't one to give up. He kept applying, and eventually he was given a break.

L.W. Bailey owned ranches throughout the West in Wyoming, Colorado, and Texas. He had a large property outside Rock River that ran a cow/calf operation. When Dale applied, this ranch was up for sale. Mr. Bailey wasn't having any luck with the business, and told Dale he would give him a year of managing it. It would stay on the market during that time, but Dale was responsible for daily operations and keeping the ranch running.

It was just what Dale had been hoping for. He knew that if just given the chance, he could prove that he was capable of running a ranch. Not wanting to disappoint the one man who had faith in him, Dale resolved to be the best ranch manager in the area. The ranch was 30,000 acres and had 2,500 mother cows. Dale often had 20 hands working for him to take care of the cattle. His family was also expected to pitch in on the ranch, and they did.

Jayne was one of his best hayers, and she was out in the fields daily. Because she was so invaluable, it was important for her to have the proper tools. She had a tractor that she would use out in the meadows, but it had open sides. Jayne would wear sheepskins to stay warm and dry, but it often didn't help. Mr. Bailey knew how hard Jayne worked and how much Dale needed her help, so he bought her an 830 John Deere tractor with a cab to keep her dry. He told her it was hers and she could do whatever she wanted with it. She called it "Big John."

The starting motor on the tractor didn't work right, and Dale never had time to work on it. To start it in the mornings, they had to pull it or let it slide down an incline and Dale told her that during the day she was never supposed to shut it off because she wouldn't get it started again. Every night she brought it in and Dale serviced it for her, then set it up on a ramp so when she was ready to start it the next day she could.

Lunch on the ranch wasn't a formal affair, and it was often placed in the crockpot so people could go to the house and eat when their schedules permitted. Very rarely did anyone eat together. But one day, Lance, Dale and Jayne's oldest son, was getting ready to head to the service and asked his mom to join him for lunch before he left. She was happy to comply.

Dale had been out irrigating, and on his way to the house, he noticed her tractor sitting in the field. It wasn't running. He went to the house to ask what had happened and Jayne explained that she completely forgot and shut it off. Dale told her she had to go start it, and Lance said he would start it for her, but they couldn't. Using a couple Jeeps and a few other trucks on the ranch, they tried to pull it through the wet meadow to get it started, but nothing was strong enough to get it rolling.

Dale rarely had new vehicles on the ranch. They weren't necessarily practical for the amount of work they had to do, but at that time, Dale had his first new truck. He had taken the back bumper off and replaced it with a modified one that would be tough enough to perform duties on the ranch. Made out of iron and welded directly to the frame, it could handle pulling anything Dale needed it to pull and couldn't be jerked off the truck. His truck was the only truck that was strong enough to get Big John moving.

No one was allowed to drive the truck except Dale, and he grabbed all the ropes and chains that he could find and headed out to the field. The tractor only needed to be pulled about 10 or 15 feet to start, and he knew he could accomplish that. He hooked up the tractor while Jayne climbed into the cab.

"What gear do I put it in?" she hollered out the window.

Irritated because he had to take time out of his day to help, he responded, "What do you think? The highest gear you got."

The highest gear on the tractor was "Road" gear, which would allow the tractor to run up to 35 miles per hour. They never used this gear because the tractor never went on the road, and in hindsight, Dale figured he should have blocked it off, but he didn't. And that was the highest gear, so that was what Jayne put the tractor in.

Dale climbed into his truck and moved forward. The tractor's tires started rolling, black smoke came out of the stack, and Dale knew he had it going. He kicked his truck into neutral, and then the biggest explosion he ever heard hit him. He was pushed forward at 25 miles per hour, and then when the truck was stopped by the end of the chain, Dale was slammed into the steering wheel, which left a perfect imprint on his chest. The tractor had ran into the back of his brand new truck at 30 miles per hour. Jayne was able to stop Big John, but not before the impact.

At that point, Dale was livid. He ran to the tractor, calling her names, but Ade, their daughter, had locked the cab doors so he couldn't get in. He told her that she tore up his new truck, but she argued she hadn't. Dale went and looked, and the only thing that happened was the bumper got slightly scratched.

Jayne was so talented with her tractor and the work she did on the ranch, some hands refused to work with her. Part of her duties included raking the fields. Her job was to follow behind the mowers, but she would always fall behind because she only had an 8-ft rake attached to the back. She asked Dale to do something to help her, so he put two of them together. This allowed her to keep up with the mowers and even get ahead of them. Often she would run into a field that hadn't yet been mowed and pull grass. She would tell them that they needed to stay out of her way, and they wouldn't speak to her. They told Dale they needed another mower, which he got, and then Jayne would fall behind again. She again asked him to help her out, so Dale put three rakes together, and she gave them hell again. After that, they got a swather that cut the grass with the mowers, and she fell behind again. The last rake Dale made for her was 36 ft long.

One day, Dale told one of his ranch hands to take the 36-ft rake into a field. The ranch hand went down to do as he was told, but came back after a few minutes.

"What gate do you want me to take that through?" he asked Dale.

"The one right there where you got the rake settin'," Dale responded.

The man looked at him in disbelief. "That's only half as big as that rake."

"So what? Even my wife can put that thing through there."

"I'd like to see that. I don't think that's so."

Dale grabbed Jayne and asked her to put the rake through the gate. She went down, put half of it through the gate, stepped on the brake, put it in reverse, and backed it through there.

The ranch hand was flabbergasted. "That's impossible! I don't believe it. But I want my time."

"What's a matter?" Dale asked.

"I don't want to be here where a woman can do something I absolutely can't do."

So Dale paid him his time.

Dale's duties on the ranch began before dawn and ended after dark. A typical day on the ranch for Dale depended on what season it was—breeding or calving. During breeding season, they would breed 60 cows a day for three days. When they used artificial insemination to impregnate the cattle, this meant they had to go into the field and locate the females that were in heat. The cows were inseminated either in the morning or evening, and they were marked with different colored paintballs so they knew which was which. They were then herded into the chutes where the artificial insemination took place.

During calving season, they would have to be on call 24 hours a day to help the cows with their births. The cows were moved into the calving shed so the calves could be born in a more controlled environment. Since they were artificially inseminated, Dale and the hands knew when to expect the calves, so they were prepared. If there were any complications, they had medical supplies nearby to help out. The mother and calf would stay in the shed until the calf could stand and walk on its own (usually about 2 hours), then they would be moved into the field and another would be brought in. Dale was lucky to get a few hours of sleep during this time.

After that was done, it was time to fix the equipment on the ranch. In order to ensure that Dale could enlist in the Army, he left agriculture and became a welder. This skill came in handy on the ranch, and he used it to fix or create equipment that would make his—and everyone else's—life easier or was necessary to keep the ranch running.

Being in a rural area and far from a major town, Dale and his family had to be self-sufficient. Trips to Laramie were made once a month to gather supplies, and that included grocery shopping. Today, with a paved road and reliable vehicles, Rock River is 45 minutes away from Laramie. Back in Dale's day, it would have been an all-day trip there and back. That was valuable time away from the ranch that couldn't happen often. Because the trips were made infrequently, Dale and the family stocked up on numerous groceries. They often spent hundreds of dollars and filled four or five carts in one trip. Often, they would draw a small crowd who were curious to see how much their bill would be and what they were purchasing.

Jayne was able to take these supplies and cook meals fit for a king. Dale and several others in the area really appreciated what Jayne fixed. Ranch hands and community members were thrilled to be invited into the house to eat.

And it wasn't only people who enjoyed her cooking. Wild animals also loved her meals. There had been a particular skunk that was treated to the milk gravy skillet after dinner. She named him Pepe Le Pew. He would come to the house every day and "talk" to Jayne until she gave him a treat. He was one of many that came up to the porch, and he would sit right in the middle of the pan, not allowing any of the others to eat until he got his fill. He would be so full, he would waddle away from the porch. Eventually, he stopped coming around and no one knew exactly what happened to him.

Jayne wasn't the only chef in the family; Dale also fancied himself a pretty good cook and was known to prepare supper once in a while. To this day, he enjoys cooking, and he often makes and delivers meals to those in his neighborhood who are in need.

Life on Mr. Bailey's ranch was busy, and being so far from others meant Dale and his family had to be self-reliant—and they succeeded. Being around livestock his entire life, Dale knew the animals inside and out—literally—and often had to perform medical procedures on the cows. Again, this had to do with their distance from veterinarians and the need to keep the cattle healthy. And Dale was good at it. Ranch owners from all over the region would call on him to take care of their cattle. He was both competent and cheap.

Technically, Dale wasn't supposed to perform these medical procedures on the cattle because he wasn't licensed, but when it came down to life and death, he wasn't going to stand idly by. A rancher's livelihood depends on healthy livestock, and while veterinarians visited the ranches and did their rounds, they couldn't be there *all the time*. Therefore, the ranchers adapted and did what was necessary to ensure the sustainability of their animals and their ranches.

Some of the treatments Dale performed included removing a tumor off a heifer's brisket and taking out cancer eyes. The tumor had been about the size of a basketball, and Dale was confident he could take it off, but it was a tedious process. If he cut it wrong, the cow could bleed to death. But since the cow wasn't any good with the tumor, the ranch owner was willing to take the chance. Dale got to work. After giving the cow a spinal to knock it out, he cautiously cut the tumor layer by layer. While this was going on, a *real* veterinarian was onsite conducting an inspection of cattle that were being shipped to Texas. He noticed Dale hard at work and asked who he was. When the man told him, "Oh, that's Robinson," the veterinarian responded, "I've heard about him. Supposed to be a pretty good vet." And then everyone continued on with their work. No one questioned what Dale was doing, even though technically he shouldn't have been doing it.

As for removing the cancer eye, this was something Dale had done several times in the past. More often than not, removing it didn't affect the cow in a negative way, and they went on living their lives and having calves with one eye. On one particular occasion, a fellow rancher asked Dale to remove a cancer eye from a cow. He set to work, and in a short while, the ranch owner asked him how everything was going.

"Great!" Dale told him. "This is the best cow I've ever operated on. She's been still the entire time."

The rancher examined the cow, then looked at Dale. "I think that cow's dead."

"Nah. She ain't dead. She's just resting."

But then Dale took a closer look, and sure enough, the cow had died. The owner wasn't upset and commented that the cow had lived a good life.

Dale's reputation as a capable veterinarian was known far and wide, but if they hadn't seen his skills in action, some doubted the truthfulness behind the stories. One particular individual mentioned this to Mr. Bailey and said that he would like to see for himself if the stories were actually true. Mr. Bailey told him to head up to the ranch to see for himself, so he did.

That day happened to be an incredibly busy day for Dale. It was a calving day, so they had induced about 80 heifers and had to keep an eye on them as they gave birth. There also happened to be a prolapse, where the cow's uterus was hanging out of her body, so Dale had to put it back in. There was also a breech calf, which was too big to come out naturally and was hip locked, so he had to perform a C-section. He removed a cancer eye, and then he had to deal with a calf with a broken leg. The break occurred when one of the ranch hands was helping it out of the mother, and it was a compound fracture—the bone was protruding from the skin. Dale asked someone to sit on the calf so he could cut the leg off, but no one would do it. Finally, his mom was willing to help him out. She sat on the calf, Dale cut off his leg, and then put a patch over the bottom so that when it healed it could walk on it like a make-shift hoof.

The guy left the ranch, unable to handle any other medical procedures. He mailed Dale a book later and said he would have never believed Dale was capable of doing all those things if he hadn't seen it with his own eyes. He inscribed the book with: "To my OBGYN, orthopedic surgeon, and optometrist." Dale never saw the guy again, but he still has the book.

Life on the ranch could be tough, but it was what Dale had always known and all he'd ever wanted to do. If it hadn't been for L.W. Bailey, Dale might have never gotten the opportunity to manage a ranch and own his own.

CHAPTER 8:

L.W. BAILEY

L.W. Bailey was the only ranch owner in the region to give young Dale a chance at managing a ranch. After the year was up, the ranch still hadn't sold, but Mr. Bailey took it off the market. Dale had transformed it into a profitable, sustainable operation.

Dale was always grateful to Mr. Bailey, and he worked hard to prove that he had made the right decision in making Dale the manager. Dale always thought of Mr. Bailey as a father figure and spoke of him fondly. Mr. Bailey had lost a son that was about Dale's age, so there was a bond that formed between the two.

In his life, Dale never once heard Mr. Bailey say anything bad about anyone, and no one said anything bad about him. He always thought that was an amazing thing, especially considering no human was without their faults. A multimillionaire from ranches throughout the West, Mr. Bailey was an unassuming man. He lived frugally and often dressed in old clothes. To look at him, one would never believe he was worth so much. He and his wife lived in an old store building that had 8-ft partitions to create separate rooms. When Dale first started working for him, he lived in the partition next to theirs, and they were always so good to him.

During the time Dale knew Mr. Bailey, he never bought a new car. Mr. Bailey was more than happy to buy used cars, and Dale had gone with him on several trips to pick out a "new" one. One of the tests that Mr. Bailey always put the car through was to take it through a car wash. He had owned a car previously where the window leaked when it rained, so he took the other cars through a carwash to make sure all the seals were intact. He refused to have the dealership fix the window, but he wasn't going to get a broken one again.

Mr. Bailey was a charitable man. He and Dale attended machine sales where farm equipment was auctioned off. It was too expensive for most of the local ranchers to buy outright, so Mr. Bailey would buy all of it and provide it to the other ranchers there on loan. Mr. Bailey wanted to help out his fellow ranchers, so he never made them sign contracts, it was all done on a handshake and a word, and Dale didn't think he ever lost a penny on any of the deals.

Mr. Bailey enjoyed helping out his fellow ranchers. There was one time when Mr. Bailey and Dale had gone into a bank and the loan officer was upset about the agricultural loans. Mr. Bailey told him that he was more than willing to take the worst offenders off the bank's hands. The loan officer was shocked and exclaimed, "You'll break the bank!" He wasn't allowed to buy the loans, despite his offer to do so.

Mr. Bailey was determined to make sure that Dale had all the skills and knowledge he needed to be the best ranch manager around, so for 2 months out of the year, he would send Dale down to Kansas to participate in seminars. Dale's father always said he was going down there to "poop around" while the rest of them were stuck working, but he was actually learning the business. Dale learned how to put up 4 tons of hay per acre while everyone else around him was putting up 1 ton to the acre. He also was taught how to get his calves from 300+ pounds to more than 600 pounds.

It was at these seminars that Dale learned about artificial insemination for cows. It was a 2-week course that started at 6:30 in the morning and went until 7:00 at night. This would prove to be beneficial for Dale later down the road. The practice was interesting to him, and he had the basic knowledge to start, but he wore himself out trying to get it just right. Eventually, that led him to a relationship with Colorado

State University and scientific breakthroughs in the field, which are discussed in chapter 9.

After the first year, Dale was no longer attending the seminars in Kansas, he was leading them. He had vast knowledge about the ranching industry and was willing to share it with others. His hope was that it would give them the opportunity to be as successful as he was.

The relationship between Dale and Mr. Bailey was mutually beneficial. Mr. Bailey gave him every opportunity to be the best, and Dale always had Mr. Bailey's best interests in mind and did what he had to do to keep the ranch running smoothly and efficiently—but that often didn't endear him to other ranchers in the area. One of the biggest fights Dale found himself in with others was over water. It was an argument that surfaced over and over and wasn't unique to Dale and the ranch. Since ranchers settled in Wyoming, water rights have always been a bone of contention.

In a nutshell, Wyoming water laws, which date back to territorial days, are based on the "doctrine of prior appropriation," which means that the first person to put the water to beneficial use has the first right. This means that water rights in the state are regulated by priority. However, just because someone has first rights, that doesn't mean they own the water. According to the Wyoming Constitution, all natural streams, springs, lakes, and other collections belong to the state.[1]

Wyoming has been divided into four divisions, which are managed by the State Engineer. The water in each division is administered by a superintendent with assistance from water and hydrographer commissioners. These four superintendents and the State Engineer make up the state board of control.[1]

There are different types of water in Wyoming—surface and ground—and both of them have different laws that apply. Surface water laws were first enacted in 1875, but more comprehensive laws were written into the state constitution and adopted in 1890. Groundwater laws were enacted in 1945 and amended in 1947. In 1958, a new groundwater law went into effect on March 1, which repealed and replaced the 1945 and 1947 laws. In 1969, more major amendments were made. These laws are incredibly detailed and comprehensive, much more than needs to go into this book, but in essence, if anyone (an individual, association, or corporation) wants to use surface or ground water, they have to apply for a permit with the State Engineer and adhere to the process that follows.[1]

Water is one of the most important elements of survival, second to oxygen, and wars have been fought over the rights and control of water in an area. Wyoming is a dry place, but it has its share of water sources. These have often been the site of many disputes. As early as 1983, there were cases in the courts about water rights. These included *Frank v. Hicks, McPhail v. Forney*, and *Moyer v. Preston*.[1] Litigation measures carried throughout the years, reshaping and redefining water rights throughout Wyoming. What Dale experienced during his time on Mr. Bailey's ranch was typical for the area.

While working for Mr. Bailey, Dale was president of the ditch company. His job was to help resolve water issues among ranchers, and he often took a firm and unwavering stance on the matter—that didn't always agree with what others wanted. But Dale wouldn't be swayed. They would have local meetings and the other ranchers would never say anything inside, but as soon as they got outside, they would get into groups and lodge their complaints with one another. Dale noticed this and asked them repeatedly to bring their issues inside where they could be taken care of, but they always told him nothing was wrong.

Dale explains that he was really lucky to have Don Sims as a water commissioner and a neighboring rancher. The Sims were good friends and neighbors, and Mary Sims and Jayne were probably the best ranch women in the entire area. The Sims had the Valley Station near McFadden, which was a gathering place for many locals to take their families for dances and fun. In the trees in the back was a rodeo ground where the locals competed for bragging rights. To this day, the Sims have a successful ranching business in the same area.

Eventually, Dale made a trip down to the State Engineer's Office and tabulated the water rights of the area. After that happened, no one had anything to fight about, so they stopped attending the meetings altogether. But before Dale was armed with that information, there was plenty of discord to go around.

One night after dinner, Mr. Bailey called Dale into his office. Mr. Bailey owned a large roll-top desk, and he slid the top back and pulled out a stack of papers. They were letters from unhappy ranchers in the area. They were complaining about Dale. Mr. Bailey let Dale read each letter and gave him the chance to tell his side of the story. The vast majority of the complaints dealt with the water in the area, and Dale explained they were trying to take what rightfully belonged to Mr. Bailey.

After each letter and each explanation, Mr. Bailey threw the letter away, and the matter was never brought up again. Mr. Bailey respected and appreciated that Dale kept the best interests of the ranch and his well-being forefront in his mind.

On another occasion, surveyors for a mining company would come onto the property to search for oil. There are many ways to search for oil and gas underground, and one of those ways includes seismology. Shock waves are sent into the rock layers beneath the surface and the waves bounce back to the surface. "The reflections travel at different speeds depending upon the type or density of rock layers through which they must pass. Sensitive microphones or vibration detectors detect the reflections of the shock waves—hydrophones over water, seismometers over land. Seismologists interpret the readings for signs of oil and gas traps."[2] Once oil or gas is found, it is marked on a GPS so that the mining company can come and collect the valuable minerals.

The mining company came onto the property to conduct seismographs without any compensation to Mr. Bailey, and Dale wouldn't stand for it. When the company came in to do their seismographs, Dale stopped them and said, "From now on, you're going to come by our house and you're going to pay $35 a hole."

At first, the company said no because they had the mineral rights. Dale pointed out that they didn't have ingress and egress, and he would hold up their operations if they didn't comply. While Dale couldn't deny them the ability to drill on the land, he could hamper their ability to enter and exit the ranch—he had control over that. He also had the right to charge the company for access to the land.

"Do you know what it would cost you to hold this outfit up?" the company man asked.

"No. How much?" Dale wondered.

"It would cost several thousand dollars a day."

"Then $35 a hole won't hurt you much, will it?" Dale pointed out.

This, of course, upset the company man and he told Dale that he had no way to do it, so Dale called him on his bluff. He started writing down their license plate numbers and reported them to the deputy sheriff.

"Don't move these vehicles 'til I tell you it's clear," the deputy sheriff told the company men.

This got them worried. He begged the deputy sheriff not to shut them down and told him that he would present this to his company and work it out.

Dale told the deputy sheriff to give them 5 days to see what they could do. The company was given 5 days to work, then if nothing came of it, he would shut them down.

Energy has always played an important role in Wyoming. The state provides more energy to the nation than any other state.[3] Wyoming has 23 counties, and all but one produces either coal, oil, or natural gas.[4] Mineral royalties, severance, and related energy taxes are a major portion of state revenues.[4]

In the late 1860s, coal deposits in southern Wyoming influenced the Union Pacific to lay its track through the state.[5, 6] This helped develop the Wyoming Territory in 1868 because the railroad created communities and industry. When the railroads switched to diesel engines in 1950, coal production dropped significantly.[7,8] However, it bounced back in the 1960s when coal-burning, steam-powered generating plants were constructed in Glenrock and Kemmerer.[9] Then, there was a high demand for low-sulfur coal from the Powder River Basin in the 1970s.[9] By 1985, Wyoming became the largest coal-producing state in the country—and it still holds that title today.[10, 11]

Wyoming is the national leader of coal production.[4] In 2012, it contributed 39 percent of all coal.[12] The state also holds more than one-third of the recoverable coal reserves in the U.S. and has eight of the largest coal mines in the country.[4]

Oil became the state's most valuable energy resource in the 1920s because of the growing popularity of automobiles and the need for gasoline, but production of oil began in the 1880s.[13, 14] Back then, the most significant oil field was the Salt Creek Oil Field in northern Natrona County.[15, 16] Oil continued to be prosperous until the 1930s when the Great Depression took its toll on the nation.[16] WWII revitalized the industry and production continued to increase until 1970, when it peaked.[16] For the next 20 years, the industry didn't do so well, and many refineries closed.[16] Today, oil production has once again become vital to the state economy, but it hasn't reached past production levels.[16]

Another industry that is a valuable resource in Wyoming is natural gas. Major discoveries of the gas took place in the 1970s in the Overthrust Belt of southwestern Wyoming,[11, 17] then there was a major boom in Sublette County near Pinedale in the 1990s and early 2000s.[18] This led to the development of the Jonah Field and the Pinedale Anticline.[18] Even though it had been mined before, new drilling techniques and fracturing technology made it possible to get to gas deposits that couldn't be accessed previously.[18]

As the fifth leading producer of natural gas,[3] Wyoming ranks in the top 10 natural gas-producing states in the nation.[4] The Pinedale and Jonah fields in the state are among the top 10 largest natural gas fields in the nation.[4] Most of the production occurs in the southwest part of the state, and federal lands produce two-thirds of Wyoming's natural gas.[4]

Uranium and wind energy also play a role in the energy industry of Wyoming.[4] Uranium was first discovered near Lusk in 1918[19] and boomed in the 1950s and 1960s, and demand is growing again.[20] For wind, Wyoming has some of the highest sustained winds in the continental U.S., so we are an excellent location for wind turbines.[4] Early wind farms cropped up in the 1980s, and now larger turbines can be seen throughout the state.[21]

Wyoming, like many other areas in the Rocky Mountain West, have split estates, which means that the surface rights can be privately owned while the subsurface mineral rights are federally owned. This occurred when the Stock Raising Homestead Act of 1916 was passed by Congress. Settlers could claim 640 acres of nonirrigable land designated by the Secretary of the Interior and "stock raising," but the government retained rights to the minerals. The landowner owns the surface and is allowed to develop these lands by developing water sources and infrastructures associated with grazing and foraging crops, but they don't have the right to sell the mineral resources.[22]

Because the government owns the vast majority of mineral rights, the Bureau of Land Management (BLM) manages the subsurface mineral rights—700 million acres of subsurface mineral estate nationwide, including approximately 58 million acres where the surface is privately owned.[23] If a company shows interest in wanting to mine on certain lands, there is a process that must be followed, along with federal laws, regulations, and BLM policy directives. According to the Split Estate Right, Responsibilities, and Opportunities brochure:

> Under these laws, regulations, and procedures, the leasing and development of Federal oil and natural gas resources occur in four phases:

- Planning and Leasing
- Permitting
- Drilling and Production
- Surface Reclamation

In each phase, the BLM, the lessee/operator, and the private surface owner have rights, responsibilities, and opportunities. Parcels of land or mineral estate open for leasing under the terms of a BLM land use plan may be nominated for leasing by companies or members of the public. The BLM reviews every nomination to ensure that leasing the parcel would conform to the terms of the land use plan, which has been developed previously with broad public input.

The initial term for a Federal oil and gas lease is 10 years, but production can extend this lease period. Successfully bidding on and acquiring the oil and gas lease gives the lessee or designated operator the right to enter and occupy as much of the surface as is reasonably required to explore, drill, and produce the oil and natural gas resources on the leasehold, subject to applicable Federal laws, regulations, lease stipulations, and permit requirements. The BLM works to encourage coordination and cooperation among all parties that have rights and responsibilities in split estate situations.[23]

The company man headed down to Denver, where company was headquartered, and explained to the company about having to pay $35 per hole to continue seismograph activity. After the 5 days were up, the company man called

Dale and said he had a check for him that he could pick up in Rock River.

Dale felt that something about the situation was off, so he grabbed his nephew Ernie, who had just been discharged from the Navy, to ride to town with him. Ernie loved to fight, so he was the perfect person to have on Dale's side if something went wrong—and Dale was convinced *something* was going to go wrong.

They went to Rock River and found the guy at his car. In his car was one of the biggest guys Dale had ever seen. He didn't have a neck because he was so muscle bound. Dale's suspicions were confirmed. He met the guy, knowing that when he went by the car, No Neck would be waiting to "massage" him. And he was right. The guy climbed out of the car and headed toward Dale, which led Ernie to jump out of Dale's car and intercept him. Ernie took the man around the block to where no one could see them. Dale was left with the company man, but he wasn't worried about him. Dale knew he could take him.

When Ernie finally came back, he looked at the company man and asked, "Now do you want a little of it?"

"No," he replied. "Not a bit."

Dale and Ernie climbed into the car to head home.

From then on, getting the $35 per hole wasn't an issue, and it made Mr. Bailey approximately $40,000 to $50,000. But the company wasn't happy about it and tried to discredit Dale. They would make the checks out to him, thinking Dale would take the money for himself, essentially embezzling from Mr. Bailey, but Dale didn't fall for it. He signed every single check over to Mr. Bailey and mailed it to him.

In many ways, Dale was the quintessential rancher. He was tough, rugged, no-nonsense, and knew livestock like the back of his hand. But underneath that gruff and weathered exterior, Dale had a soft spot. And like Mr. Bailey, he wanted to do what he could to help others and give them a chance to prove themselves worthy. He would go out of his way for friends and family—made sure they were taken care of, but he also took in troubled kids.

There's no doubt that life on the ranch with Dale was challenging. Everyone had to pull their own weight; everyone had to work. It was just what these kids needed to whip them back into shape. Dale may have been hard on them, but he also wanted them to succeed. What he gave them on the ranch was a work ethic and a sense of pride. Life is never easy, but hard work makes it pay off. After their time on the ranch, many of these kids went on to be productive members of society—two of them became highway patrolmen.

Not all off the kids who came to the ranch needed their lives straightened out, some just wanted to learn the business of ranching. A student from Iran came to Dale's ranch while he was attending Colorado State University and later became the Secretary of the Interior for Iran. He and his wife considered Dale and his family their own family. When his wife had a baby, Dale and Jayne went to visit them in the hospital, but they were told only family could enter the room. The Iranian man and his wife told the hospital staff that Jayne was the baby's grandmother, so they were allowed to go in.

Dale proved over and over again that he was a capable ranch manager. He was tough, but he made the ranch successful and profitable. As he was determined to do, Dale eventually had enough money to buy a ranch on his own. For all his hard work and dedication, Mr. Bailey rewarded Dale with property that allowed him to expand the ranch he had bought. The portion of property that Mr. Bailey gifted to Dale was 640 acres in Section 20. It was partially watered and could put up 4 tons of hay per acre. It increased Dale's ranch size to 1,404 acres and allowed him to run and sell 325 cows. His dream was finally fulfilled.

This ranch wasn't the only property Mr. Bailey wanted to give Dale. On one occasion, Mr. Bailey and Dale made a trip to the lawyer's office in Rawlins. Mr. Bailey was working on incorporating his ranches in Wyoming and Colorado. As they were leaving, the lawyer told Dale that he wanted to have a word with him. Mr. Bailey excused himself outside.

"You know he wants to give you that ranch, don't you?" the lawyer asked.

"Yeah, I do," replied Dale.

"Why don't you take it? It's a five-million-dollar ranch!"

Dale explained that he knew that, but if he were to take it, he would make it the best ranch on the creek—better than it was now—and kill himself in the process. He and Jayne wanted to get away from the ranching life and enjoy themselves and play a little.

Not only did Dale make Mr. Bailey's ranch successful, but he was determined to do the same with his own. He was given the opportunity to hand pick his own cattle to populate his ranch with. He chose some black and whites (what ranchers refer to as "black baldies") and started with 50 head. It didn't take long for Dale's ranch to be just as successful and thriving as Mr. Bailey's—it was just a bit smaller.

Photos of Dale's former ranch in Rock River, Wyoming (taken by Jessica Robinson).

CHAPTER 9:

ADVANCING THE SCIENCE OF RANCHING

Along with his veterinary skills, Dale had vast knowledge about artificial insemination (AI) for cows. He wanted his ranch and the ranch he managed to be successful, so he was incredibly particular about his cattle. He only bred them with the best. He was also always looking for ways to improve the AI process, and that led him to forming a relationship with Colorado State University (CSU).

The Morrill Act of 1862 and the Hatch Act of 1887 were instrumental in the founding of CSU. The Morrill Act provided each state with 30,000 acres of federal land for each member in their Congressional delegation for them to sell and use the proceeds to fund public colleges that focused on agriculture and the mechanical arts. It was sponsored by Vermont Congressman Justin Morrill and signed into law by President Lincoln on July 2, 1862.[1] The Hatch Act supplied federal funds to land-grant colleges so they could create agricultural stations and pass on new information in the areas of soil minerals and plant growth. The bill was named from Congressman William Hatch, who had been the chair of the House Committee of Agriculture.[2] According to the act, the experiment stations were supposed to "conduct original and other research, investigations and experiments bearing directly on and contributing to the establishment and maintenance of a permanent and effective agricultural industry..."[3]

CSU was founded in 1870 as the Colorado Agricultural College.[4] It is a land-grant university that is ranked among the nation's leading research universities. The Colorado

Agricultural Experiment Station was established in 1888. Like Wyoming, the climate of Colorado is variable, and there are various types of farms and ranches that try to sustain a living. The scientific expertise and research capabilities of the faculty at CSU helps farmers and ranchers in the state "enhance profitability, protect the environment, sustain natural resources and improve the well-being of rural Colorado and all consumers."[5]

One of the things that the researchers from CSU found so appealing about Dale was his advanced techniques. That, and since he wasn't a licensed veterinarian, he had more freedom to experiment with AI techniques in his cattle, and he was willing to work with professors and graduate students on his ranch.

The head professor that Dale worked with on the AI project was Dr. B.W. Pickett. Dr. Pickett first came to CSU in 1967, and in 1971 became director of the Animal Reproduction Laboratory (ARL) where he oversaw "some of the monumental breakthroughs in animal reproductive science, including the first set of cloned twin calves in 1982 and the country's first 'man-made' identical twin foals from one split embryo in 1984."[6] He also developed and became the first director of CSU's Equine Reproduction Laboratory.

Dr. Pickett became director of Equine Sciences in 1982. He was the driving force behind one of the nation's first equine teaching and research centers. As of 2000, the lab was "the largest and most productive equine teaching, research and service program in the world."[6] By combining all horse programs across all colleges at CSU, he was also responsible for the creation of the first equine science major. CSU was the first university to offer this type of program.

Dr. Pickett has received several honors in his long career, including the American Society of Animal Science's Physiology and Endocrinology Award for outstanding research in reproductive physiology and the National Association of Animal Breeders Research Award in recognition of meritorious research contribution in the field of animal reproduction and artificial insemination.[6]

CSU presented him the L.W. Durrell Distinguished Service Award in recognition of excellence in research and creativity, and he received the Distinguished Service Award from the Equine Nutrition and Physiology Society in 1981, and the Colorado Horseman's Council also named him Colorado Horseman of the Year.[6]

Dale first met Dr. Pickett when he came to CSU to have some bull semen frozen. They went to lunch and talked about ranching and how AI was used very rarely on ranches. Dr. Pickett was confused as to why beef cattle weren't being bred with AI because "In 1967, over 70 percent of the dairy cows in the United States were being bred utilizing AI, compared to 3-5 percent of the beef cattle."[7] Dale had been breeding all the cows on his property for several years, but this gave him and the professors the opportunity to improve the process and conduct experiments. In Dr. Pickett's mind, using AI was the best way to improve the genetic merit of Dale's herds.

He visited the ranch and after long discussions with Dale, they decided that they would like to work with Dale and his cows. The stipulation was that "ARL personnel could conduct experiments, on such topics as heterospermic insemination, estrous cycle synchronization, induction of calving, and post-partum anestrus, to name a few."[7] Dr. Pickett would supply all of the labor and semen, and Dale was more than happy to comply. According to Dr. Pickett:

> This agreement with Mr. Robinson was truly a 'marriage made in heaven.' Personnel at ARL began breeding these cows in 1971 and stopped after the 1979 breeding season. When they started, the calving interval was 120 days; in 1979, it was between 30 and 45 days. In 1971, the pregnancy rate was 84%; in 1979, the pregnancy rate was 97%. During this period,

weaning weights increased from 340 to 540 lbs. Much of the increase in weaning weights was due to the fact that a drug company had purchased a local bull stud and was delighted to supply us with all the frozen semen we wanted for any of their bulls, provided that we would give them the weaning weight of each calf to aid in proving their bulls. Further, they would pay a few cents more per pound for those calves, which were destined to go into their feedlot.[8]

The first day Dr. Pickett spent on the ranch with Dale began early, before 6:00 a.m. They were heading over to Section 20 to set the water before coming back to get started. They drove to the junction of Highway 287 and Wyoming 13 in Rock River and stopped at the service station sign, and Dale looked around. At this point, it was exactly 6:00 a.m.

"I hired two guys yesterday," said Dale, "and they were supposed to be here at exactly six o'clock."

But they weren't. So they headed to Section 20 to set the water, then they came back 20 to 30 minutes later. The two guys were standing there. Dale got out of the truck and walked up to them.

"Where were you at six o'clock?" he asked.

They responded, "Well, we were just a little bit late."

"I can tell you this, I don't need anyone that can't show up on time. You're fired." And Dale climbed back into the truck.

There were many adventures beyond that, including ranch hands that often tried to get the better of Dr. Pickett.

Heat checks would begin at daylight. Those cows to be bred would be marked with paint balls fired from pellet guns, one color for evening and another color for morning breeding. Of the five or six graduate students who would participate the first year, only two could ride a horse, and had some experience moving cattle. The first year alone could have provided sufficient comedy and drama to sustain a 10-season soap opera written by Baxter Black. Those Wyoming cowboys would have a little fun with a college professor at every opportunity. They had in their pay a horse named Goosey who was given to Dr. Pickett to ride without the benefit of an entirely forthcoming introduction. 'The first day, after having ridden all day, in that moment between when I had already gone off clock and had not yet dismounted in the normal way, Goosey earned his under-the-table pay. He threw me as high as the reins would let me go. My heels and the back of my head hit the gravel road at the same time. Lying there, looking at the sky, I very distinctly remember thinking, "We only have 59 more days to go".' One of our graduate students, who was an excellent AI technician, but not even as good a 'cowboy' as yours truly, got a horse on 'high center' in an irrigation ditch. After the first week, Mr. Robinson expressed the fervent hope that what he had seen thus far would not be reflected in the pregnancy rates. We may not have been the best cowboys, but we could breed cows in estrus under almost any conditions. Fortunately, the ranches had excellent facilities for handling, sorting, and breeding range cattle.[7]

Another ARL researcher that also conducted experiments with Dale on his ranch was George Seidel. For his work, Dr. Seidel has received numerous awards, including the Alexander von Humboldt Award, National Association of Animal Breeders Research Award, Upjohn Physiology Award,

American Dairy Science Association, University Distinguished Professor Faculty Distinguished Service Award, Gamma Sigma Delta, Honorary Lifetime Membership in the American Embryo Transfer Association and the International Embryo Transfer Society (IETS) Distinguished Service Award, and the IETS Pioneer Award. He was elected to the US National Academy of Science in 1992.[9]

Dr. Seidel was raised on a dairy farm in Pennsylvania, and he received his bachelor's degree from Penn State in Dairy Science in 1965. He received his master's and doctoral degrees from Cornell University in 1968 and 1970, respectively. He did postdoctoral studies at Harvard Medical School, where he studied rabbit oocytes with electron microscopy before coming to CSU as an assistant professor. He became a University Distinguished Professor, and even though he has "retired," he still has lab space on campus and does guest lectures for classes.[10]

According to the biography that was written by Dr. Seidel for his 2008 IETS Pioneer Award,

> Over the past 20 years, Dr Seidel's research program has focussed increasingly on basic science. His studies have included groundbreaking work in oocyte maturation, in vitro fertilisation, and culture of bovine and equine embryos. During the past decade, Dr Seidel has made a huge effort in developing methods for sex selection of sperm and applying this technology to livestock production. The procedures were refined for sexing sperm rapidly with ~90% accuracy. A key to applying this technology was developing low-dose artificial insemination procedures; under some circumstances, fertility is only slightly lower with a dose of two million frozen bovine sperm compared with the more conventional

insemination doses of 10–20 sperm. This research has led to commercialisation of sexed semen for artificial insemination of cattle worldwide.[9]

The relationship between Dale and Dr. Seidel started with "exotic" breeds from Europe, which include Simmentals and Limousin. Compared to the cattle in Wyoming, which were Herefords and Angus, the "exotic" breeds were larger and meatier. Importation of them from Europe started in the late 1960s/early 1970s. The exotics were mixed with the standard Wyoming breeds, but since they were larger, they resulted in more birth difficulties, especially for first-calf heifers. Experiments were conducted mostly by Dr. Ed Carroll, an ARL veterinarian, on inducing calving, both to make it easier on the heifer with the large calf and to test various methods. This experiment accomplished two things: making the calves smaller and allowing the scientists and ranchers to be there for the births.

Dr. Seidel, along with an ARL veterinarian, Dr. Peter Elsden, also conducted experiments on the ranch that included transferring freshly collected embryos nonsurgically and transferring frozen embryos into cows. These were new and groundbreaking experiments. The outcome of this work included simplifying embryo freezing procedures and higher pregnancy rates with the methods that were used. Dr. Seidel is given credit for his work on cattle transferring to work that was done to help infertile human couples. The experiments with cattle transferred to how to work with human embryos. These experiments also helped in the management of difficult pregnancies.

Another goal of the experiments was to raise a calf that weighed half as much as its mother by the time it was weaned. This meant if the mother weighed 1,000 pounds, the calf would have to weigh 500 pounds, or else it would be sold. The calves that made their weight were kept on the ranch to be bred.

How much a cow weighs dictates how much they are worth on the market. A larger calf means that it will have more meat to be sold on the market, which is why the exotic breeds were important. Since they were bigger, they were more economically viable—both to the rancher and the consumer. The experiments were conducted to figure out ways to make it easier for the Wyoming cattle to be interbred with the exotics and have larger calves. Inducing labor a few weeks earlier in first-calf heifers made the calves smaller, which in turn made the delivery easier.

According to Dale, these calves would be about 18 pounds lighter than full-term calves. The goal was to regain this weight as the calf grew, but it never did. It was always lighter than other calves born at the same time. However, because it was an exotic, it was still larger on average than the standard breeds in Wyoming.

The weight trials and experiments were conducted by Dr. Jim Waggoner, a professor from the University of Wyoming (UW), and his graduate students. Like CSU, UW is a land-grant university. It was founded in 1886—before Wyoming was even a state.[11] UW is the state's only 4-year institution. The mission of the College of Agriculture and Natural Resources "is to be the proactive leader in education and scholarship to cultivate healthy, sustainable systems for Wyoming's agriculture, environment and natural resources, and rural communities. Our vision is to serve people through the application of the land grant principles of learning, engagement, and discovery."[12]

Dr. Waggoner first met Dale and Jayne at an agricultural banquet. After speaking with a supplemental feed supplier about testing some of their products, Dr. Waggoner approached Dale later and asked if he could conduct some experiments, and Dale agreed.

Dr. Waggoner grew up on a small cow-calf, yearling operation in central New Mexico. He received his bachelor and master's degree from New Mexico State University in range animal nutrition and management. His Ph.D. is from the University of Illinois in beef cattle management and nutrition with a minor in forage crops. He came to UW directly after graduating with his Ph.D. to be a professor in beef cattle management as it relates to range livestock production. He has been an associate professor for the past 36 years and has written or contributed to 25 articles related to the cattle industry.[13]

One of the experiments that was conducted involved a liquid winter feed that was mostly molasses. The cows involved in this research were 2 year olds on Mr. Bailey's ranch and calves that had just been weaned on Dale's ranch. The molasses concoction was placed in a container with a lick wheel that turned as the cows licked it, coating it with more molasses. The 2 year olds had no problems with the set up. Part of the reason for this was because they spent the winter in the barn and were corralled. They could easily get to the supplemental feed tub, which was protected from the weather by the corral fences. The calves, however, weren't as lucky.

The calves didn't always have the tongue strength to turn the wheel. Another issue was that the calves weren't corralled in a barn, so the molasses mixture would get very cold since the feeding tub was out in the pasture and exposed to the winter weather. Determined to make sure they got results from the research, they took a suggestion from a local ranch supply store owner to take the lid off the top of the tank and place some weighted pallets in the molasses. There would be a few inches of molasses on top of the pallets, and the calves would be able to access it easily. This was even more disastrous than the lick wheel. On several occasions, a calf would fall into the tank and have to be fished out.

"If you've never fished a 450- or 500-pound heifer covered in molasses out of a 500-gallon molasses tank, you've never had a living experience," explains Dr. Waggoner.

The calves and the humans would be coated in the sticky feed. However, the calves would then become the most popular calf in the field. Because this part of the experiment was such a disaster, they eventually ended up cancelling the calf part of the study.

Another weight experiment that Dr. Waggoner conducted on Dale's ranch also involved molasses, but this time it was poured into a cardboard box and allowed to harden. The practice began in Australia and involved lining a cardboard box with a plastic bag, then pouring in the hot molasses mixture where it would solidify into a cube. The problem with this procedure was the plastic bag. It would get intertwined with the molasses. Since it was dangerous for the cows to ingest the plastic, each block had to have the plastic skinned off it before it could be fed to the cows. This took a large amount of time to get it out of the feed—time that was needed for other chores on the ranch.

After struggling to remove the plastic from the molasses blocks, Dale finally asked if it could be packaged another way—namely without the bag. Dr. Waggoner said he wasn't sure, but he would look into it. He knew the distributor in the U.S. The process was expensive and finding a replacement for the plastic and cardboard box created a major problem. Eventually, they found a box manufacturer who agreed to work with them, and the result was that the box became part of the block when the molasses was placed in it and hardened. The cattle then ate the box along with the block of hardened molasses. Now all the ranchers had to do was open the box and toss it out for the cows. Since the box was just cellulose, it wouldn't hurt them to ingest. Using soy-based inks, the companies could even print their logo on the box and it wouldn't harm the cows.

The first year of this experiment was rocky, especially with the need to "skin" the plastic bags off the blocks, but once the packaging process was changed, the results came rolling in. One of the most useful was that the blocks allowed producers a means of providing an adequate level of supplemental potassium throughout the winter feeding period to their cattle.

The experiment determined the most beneficial level of potassium to add to the winter supplement, and this level is the standard used in many feeding programs today.

Yet another weight experiment that was conducted on Dale's ranch involved implants for growth promotion in suckling calves. Normally, these were placed at the base of the calf's ear. After slaughter, the head would be used to make cheap feed for various industries, including the fur industry. Minks would eat the feed produced from the cows' heads and because the implant was in this part of the body, it was causing them to go sterile, and that was problematic. Dr. Waggoner suggested moving the implant site down the ear about 1.5 to 2.0 inches from where the base of the ear attaches to the skull of the calf. He had the ability to test this theory on Dale's calves, and the results were surprising. Results showed that calves implanted with the growth promotion implants gained 0.5 pound more per day than nonimplanted calves. The change in implant site made the animal's head more appealing for use in other animal foods as the ears could be cut off at the base of the head and disposed of (thus removing the implant site) before the heads were processed into animal food. The ears could be thrown away or used as fertilizer and it wouldn't cause any ill effects. This experiment changed how implants were placed, and today it is recommended that they go further up the ear rather than closer to the base of the skull.

Without Dale's consent and accommodations for these experiments to be conducted, science may not have reached these advancements in weight gain for cattle. Dale's foresight and collaboration helped advance scientific understandings and practices.

Dr. Waggoner claims that "What Dale provided and what we were able to do with what he provided had some major impacts on how things are done in agriculture today as it relates to growth implants—whether you like 'em or not, we had a major impact on it—and mineral supplementation, primarily the potassium level in livestock feeds."

A lot of the work conducted on Dale's ranch was published in scientific journals and made available to veterinarians and others who read these articles. Professors and graduate students alike were given hands-on opportunities to conduct experiments in real-world settings. Dale was happy and proud to be part of the research and was happy to open his land up to science. Although, there were also challenges.

Dale was tolerant of the graduate students. He realized that many of them weren't as seasoned a rancher as he was, but he also took every opportunity he could to teach them lessons about life on the ranch. One of these involved antibiotics after the cows gave birth. Dale always gave his cows a massive shot of various antibiotics after the cows gave birth to help fight infection. He had a clipboard in the birthing shed to chart when the shots were given, and the graduate students were in charge of making sure the information was up to date. Dale noticed that several of the cows had swelling in their vulvas, so he asked the students if they had been given their shots. They assured him they had. After five cows died, the students came clean and admitted they neglected to give them their shots. It was a valuable and harsh lesson for the students to learn.

Dale's contribution to this scientific research was not only allowing work to be done on his ranch and cattle, but he also participated in conferences and gave presentations. The goal was to get more ranchers interested in these techniques by having a rancher explain how beneficial they are. Dale approached Dr. Pickett for help with his presentation and to get slides to enhance it. Dr. Pickett was more than happy to assist. It was also a chance for Dr. Pickett to get some revenge for the tricks that were played on him at the ranch.

Dale ran through his speech with Dr. Pickett, who was helpful in offering feedback. He told him that in the middle of his speech, when he was talking numbers, he was going to bore the audience out of their mind. Dale needed something to wake them back up. Dr. Pickett's solution to the problem was a questionable slide. While their stories differ slightly on exactly what the slide looked like, one thing remained constant: it was a picture of a heavy-set woman without a stitch of clothes on.

"I can't put that in there," Dale told Dr. Pickett.

"Are you sure?" Dr. Pickett asked. "It'll keep your audience awake."

Dale was sure. He wasn't going to have that slide in his presentation. And Dr. Pickett didn't say anything else about it. He told Dale that he had a bull he wanted him to look at and that his assistant would put the presentation materials in Dale's car, so they headed off.

Dale didn't think anything else about the slides or the presentation. He had work to do on the ranch. When it came time for him to do his presentation, the slide wheel was waiting for him in the back of his car; right where it had been left the week before.

The presentation at the University of Wyoming was given to a packed house of about 1,000 people. Dr. Pickett had sent two of his graduate students to sit in on the presentation. They took a seat right in the front row.

Dale went through his speech and had the audience engrossed. They were hanging on his every word and enthralled with his slides. When he reached the end of his speech, he left the projector on what he thought was the last slide.

What Dale didn't realize was that the graduate students in the front row had a job besides being moral support. Dr. Pickett told them that if Dale didn't click through to the last slide, they were supposed to do it. And they did. The slide of the large, naked woman was illuminated on the screen for everyone to see. This drew hoots, hollers, and cheers from the crowd. Dale had always assumed that he had inadvertently clicked through to the last slide—and he was never sure why he would have done it—but Dr. Pickett admitted he had his student do it. Dale hated that slide, but it didn't diminish the important work that had been done on his ranch to advance AI. If anything, the end of his presentation was memorable, but it left Dale with a red face.

CHAPTER 10:

LIFE AFTER THE RANCH

In 1982, Dale sold the ranch and he and his family moved into Laramie. By this time, Mr. Bailey had lost his battle with cancer, and Dale knew that if he stayed on the ranch, he would work himself to death. He and Jayne wanted to do some traveling while they were young enough to enjoy it.

Jayne had her heart set on visiting Europe. Her stepfather had been a carpenter in Hawaii, so she spent the last 2 years of high school on the island, so she didn't want to visit there. Dale kind of wanted to see it. He wasn't overly excited about going back to Europe. He'd been there before, under different circumstances that were seared in his brain. It was difficult for him to face what he'd seen and experienced in the war, even though he knew this trip would be different. Because Jayne wanted to go, Dale took her.

When Dale managed the ranch for Mr. Bailey and then had his own, he and Jayne never had a chance to travel. There was always too much work to be done. After the ranch sold, they had nothing holding them back. They took a bus tour across Europe, then crossed the channel into France on a hovercraft that bounced across the water at 45 to 50 mph. Once in France, they visited Belgium, Luxemburg, and Paris.

Even though Dale had left the ranching life behind, that didn't mean he left agriculture altogether. He started a business evaluating ranches. For this job, Dale would answer the question: how many pounds of forage does it take to make a pound of red meat? To find the answer, Dale would evaluate how much an acre of land would produce in forage. He knew how much a cow ate by her weight, so he would use that to calculate how much forage was on the ranch and come up with a value. The more technical side of the equation is Dale would figure the carry capacity of a cow unit with the amount of forage per acre to calculate how much forage is produced by how much the cows weigh.

He also worked for the Achilles Cattle Company, who were in the business of selling bull sperm for AI breeding purposes. They dealt in Simmentals, which was a breed that came from Europe.

> The Simmental breed is sweeping the North American continent like a prairie fire and is destined to be in the very near future one of the major breeds of cattle in America.

> Their adaptability to all climatic conditions in North American plus their unequalled crossing ability on all North American cattle is the reason that they've proven to be ideal utility cattle sought after by all North American cowmen.

> The Simmental breed when crossed with our domestic cattle has added growth and milk to them, making an ideal mother cow capable of weaning a heavier calf.

> The percentage Simmental bulls used in America today are adding pounds to the calves in the domestic herds. They have been proven to be active breeders capable of moving out, and get more cows bred. The Simmental cross steers have more growth, and therefore, are providing more pounds of red meat in a shorter period of time.[1]

The history of the breed is described in the following:

The name "Simmental" is used to describe the breed of cattle where "Simmen" refers to the valley of origin in Switzerland and "tal" means valley. Simmental, whether they are found in Switzerland, France, Austria, Germany, Russia or elsewhere, have a common ancestral background dating back to the middle ages. With the migration of Simmental cattle throughout Europe, they have acquired a variety of names such as Pie Rouge, Fleckvieh, Austrian Fleckvieh, Red and White, and many local names, but in Canada they are all considered Simmental cattle, and are eligible for registration in the Canadian Simmental herd as "SIMMENTAL".[1]

What made the breed so desirable was that when crossed with the domestic breeds in the U.S., they added pounds. Adding pounds of red meat to a cow made them worth more on the market. Achilles also claimed that while they could add weight to the calves, they didn't put any undue stress on the mother at birth. They claimed that the calves could be born at a certain weight and then gain more as they grew.

Adult breeding cows have a weight of 1,450 to 1,650 pounds and stands 53 to 56 inches high at the withers, while bulls stand about three inches taller and weigh from 2,200 to 2,800 pounds in normal condition. Rapid growth is a characteristic of the breed which has shown on test a weight gain from birth to maturity averaging 2.9 pounds per day. The Simmental is a moderately early maturing animal and is

capable of producing a 1,200-pound steer in 12
to 14 months of age.[1]

The Achilles Cattle Company wanted to give their
customers the best in breeding stock, so they "proved" their
bulls and the offspring that were produced. This was
accomplished by weighing the cows after birth and as they
grew. It was also noted in how much income they produced
when sold. A few of their cattle even won championships such
as Reserve Champion at the Canadian National Exhibition in
Toronto. The company even had the bull semen evaluated
continually, and that was supervised by Dr. Pickett at CSU.[2]

With all of Dale's knowledge about cattle and the work he
had done with AI on his ranch, he was the ideal representative
to promote and inform the ranching industry about what the
Achilles Cattle Company could do. In a way, he was a
traveling salesman and he was selling the means to bigger,
beefier cattle.

He and Jayne had the opportunity to travel all across the
United States while he worked for Achilles. They had a
wonderful time on these trips and put an average of 50,000
miles on their car every year. Because of the wear and tear on
their vehicle, they bought a brand new Cadillac every 2 years.
Dale attended various functions and met all kinds of different
ranchers and ranch owners. With his vast knowledge of cattle,
this position was ideal for him. It allowed him to stay informed
about what was happening in the ranching industry and breed
the best cattle in the business.

He was on a bank board and had been responsible for
evaluating cattle and the debt to loan for agricultural loans.
Like regular loans, the borrower has to apply for an agricultural
loan. But unlike a regular loan, an agricultural loan is tied into
the borrower's well-being and livelihood. More often than not,
the money is not only used for production, but also to raise the
productivity of resources. For example, a farmer or rancher
can't do their job if they don't have the proper equipment, but

they can't buy the equipment if they don't have the money. An AG loan makes it possible for them to obtain the necessary tools to continue their work.[3]

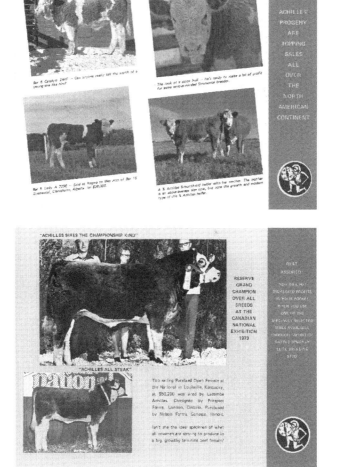

A selection of cows offered by the Achilles Cattle Company (pages taken from their catalog).

Unlike regular loans, an AG loan is not just a loan or advance, it is a means to further the well-being of the farming and ranching community. There is a complicated science behind managing the money to take scarce resources and create optimum output. Because of what farming and ranching does for society, AG loans also play an important part at the micro and macro social levels.[3]

Agricultural loans are categorized into several different levels[3]:

- Development credit or investment credit – this credit can be used to acquire durable assets or improve existing assets, including the purchasing of land or land reclamation, the purchase of farm machineries and implements, the development of irrigation facilities, the construction of farm or ranch structures, the development of plantation or orchards, and the development of animal production.
- Production credit – this credit is used for purchasing inputs and paying wages.
- Marketing credit – to get higher prices for the product, this credit is essential to carry out marketing functions.
- Consumption credit – the farmer or rancher has to meet family expenses, so this credit is used for that.
- Short-term credit – as implied in the name, this type of credit is given in periods ranging from 6 to 18 months and is intended to cover cultivation expenses, such as purchase of seed, fertilizer, pesticides, and to pay workers. Serving as the working capital so that the farm or ranch can operate efficiently, repayment is expected at the time of harvesting or marketing.
- Medium-term credit – this credit period is from 2 to 5 years and can be used for the purchase of machineries and implements or animals or for minor improvements done to the farm or ranch.
- Long-term credit – this credit term is more than 5 years up to 25 years and can be used for the purchase of big

equipment (tractors) and making permanent improvements to the ranch or farm.

Repayment of each loan depends on what type of loan it is, but they are a vital part of keeping the farming and ranching industry of the country running so that food can be put on the table. Dale helped the bank evaluate and secure $14.5 million in loans, and he evaluated cattle from South Dakota all the way to the Mexican border.

He was also a member of the Laramie Regional Airport board. Each member serves a 5-year term, but the terms are staggered so a new member starts every year. The airport was first established in 1934 and was called Brees Field.[4] It was named after U.S. Army General Herbert Jay Brees, who had been born in Laramie, Wyoming, in 1877. He graduated from the University of Wyoming with a BS in 1897 and in 1939 earned an honorary law degree. He took part in many wars, including the Spanish American War, World War I, and a small part in World War II—by that time, he had reached the mandatory retirement age in 1941.[5]

The runways on Brees Field were paved in 1944 so that hundreds of B-24 bombers could land in Laramie. They delivered crews for rest and recuperation at the University of Wyoming recreation camp in the Snowy Range. The paved runways allowed passenger service to come to the airport, and Summit Airlines began providing this service in 1945.[4]

The original terminal was built in 1959, and was remodeled in 1994. In 1992, the name of the airport changed from Brees Field to Laramie Regional Airport. Currently, the airport serves both private and corporate planes. It is also the base of the University of Wyoming's Department of Atmospheric Research aircraft, which conducts groundbreaking research. The airport plays a vital role in fire-fighting efforts and provides weather conditions for the local area. The airport is operated and financed by the City of Laramie and Albany County.[4]

Dale wasn't much for being on boards. He preferred to keep to himself. But the airport needed a businessman on their board, and after speaking to several different people who recommended that they ask Dale, they did. It took some convincing, but he finally agreed. There were moments when Dale wasn't easy to work with on the board. More often than not, the votes were 4 to 1 because he opposed them on everything. But his intentions were always noble and good. One such occasion involved the replacement of the airport's sewer system.

At first, they were told that to fix the system all they would need were three new manhole covers. Dale opposed the idea at first, but after examining the old ones and talking to the engineer, he decided to vote for the new manhole covers. He was assured that by replacing them, it would make the system like new. Three months later, the company came back to the board and told them that the entire system needed to be replaced. Dale wasn't happy. Since he had been told that the manhole covers were all that were needed, he wasn't going to vote for the new system. If the rest of the board wanted to override him, he was fine with that, but he wasn't going to say yes to the new construction.

At that same time, his niece and nephew-in-law were visiting from California. His nephew-in-law happened to be an engineer, and Dale was telling him about the new sewer system. His nephew suggested they go out and look at the system, so Dale took him out to the airport. After examining it, his nephew-in-law said that they didn't need a whole new system but they did need to change some of the pipe tie-ins and make a few bypasses. They returned to town, and the nephew-in-law drew the plans onto graph paper, telling Dale that the engineer from the construction company would have questions and how to answer them.

Dale attended the next meeting with the plans rolled up and under his arm. When asked if there was any new business, Dale said there was.

"What do you want?" they asked.

Dale told them that he was opposed to putting in a new system and that he had drawn up an idea that would fix the system and would cost a fraction of what the new system would cost. He said he would like to present it to the board, and they allowed it. Dale unrolled the papers and explained the plan. The engineer from the construction company was there, and his face from his collar to his hairline turned red. He shoved the plans to his coworker sitting next to him.

"It will work," he said. "I don't know why we didn't think about it, but it will work."

Dale's plans saved the board money, and they were able to fix the system. At the end of the meeting, the engineer from the construction company shook Dale's hand and was incredibly impressed that he was able to come up with this solution when none of their people could.

"From now on," he told Dale, "anything we have for the airport board, it will be on your desk first."

Which made Dale laugh.

Throughout his life, Dale was fortunate to meet individuals who were kind hearted and willing to help others. One of these individuals was Doug Reeves, who helped Dale through his lawsuit.

When Dale sold the ranch, he explained to the new owner that he should be able to get 4 tons of forage per acre. That had been the yield he harvested, and if the owner followed Dale's instructions exactly, his results would be the same. But for some reason, the new owner was unable to duplicate these yields, so he sued Dale.

Some of Dale's friends speculate that the reason the new owner couldn't get the same forage yield was because no one could match Dale's ability to irrigate. Living in the dry climate of Wyoming, irrigation is an important aspect in the success or failure of a ranch. As Dr. Pickett pointed out, Dale could "make water run uphill," and he had never seen anyone else with such talents for irrigation.

After the sale of the ranch, Dale wanted to invest his money, and Doug had been working for an investment firm. Doug had graduated from the University of Wyoming with a bachelor's in 1975 and a Ph.D. in 1994.

> An expert in leadership and education, Reeves founded The Leadership and Learning Center, which has offices in Boston, where Reeves lives, and Englewood, Colo. He works with education, business, nonprofit and government organizations throughout the world and has written more than 20 books and many articles on the subject. Reeves received the Brock International Award for his contributions to education and [in 2011] received the Contribution to the Field Award from the National Staff Development Council.[6]

While working for the investment firm, Doug decided he wanted to start his own investment committee. He set out on his own and asked Dale to be on the board, to which Dale agreed. While working with Doug, Dale learned a lot about investing, and he and Doug became close friends.

"He is one of the best guys I've even known," says Dale.

And to this day, the two remain in touch.

Dale's life—like anyone's—had its share of ups and downs, joys and sorrows. Unlike the average individual, when the opportunity arose for Dale to do something extraordinary, he seized it. A man from the tiny town of McFadden, Wyoming, made an impact on the world. His actions in WWII made him a hero. He served his country with honor and a sense of duty. His desire for knowledge to create high-quality cattle made him a contributor to the advancement of science.

Dale knew he was part of something special throughout the war and while assisting Drs. Pickett and Seidel. He had an inkling that his contributions were important, but at the time, he wasn't searching for glory. He was happy and willing to do what he needed to do—protect his fellow soldiers or supply the cattle for the experiments or attend seminars to impart his knowledge to others—and he did it because it was what was required of him.

Had Dale wanted, he could have demanded that his contributions to the war effort or to scientific advancement be more glorified, but that wasn't who Dale was. A humble man, he worked hard every day of his life, and the only reward he cared about was the satisfaction of a job well done.

Despite his well-known temper, Dale had a lot of friends. People admired and respected him. If Dale gave you his word, you could rest assured that he was going to carry out his promise. He always told the truth—whether the person wanted to hear it or not. As time progressed, Dale's temper and demeanor softened, but he still told the truth and continued to be a man of his word. Amazing people continue to be a part of his life, and he continues to make an impact on others.

Dale achieved his dream of owning a ranch through hard work, dedication, and never giving up. He fought through adversity and overcame obstacles. But he also achieved so much more. The world became a better place because of Dale's contributions to it. While not perfect, Dale did the best he could with the life that was given to him, and he has left a legacy for future generations to look up to and strive for.

WORKS CITED

<u>Chapter 1</u>

[1] Weidel, Nancy. *Images of America: Wyoming's Historic Ranches*. Arcadia Publishing, Charleston, South Carolina. Page 7.

[2] Weidel, Nancy. *Images of America: Wyoming's Historic Ranches*. Arcadia Publishing, Charleston, South Carolina. Page 13.

[3] Weidel, Nancy. *Images of America: Wyoming's Historic Ranches*. Arcadia Publishing, Charleston, South Carolina. Page 17.

[4] Weidel, Nancy. *Images of America: Wyoming's Historic Ranches*. Arcadia Publishing, Charleston, South Carolina. Page 21.

[5] Wikipedia. "Winter of 1886–87." https://en.wikipedia.org/wiki/Winter_of_1886%E2%80%9387

[6] Weidel, Nancy. *Images of America: Wyoming's Historic Ranches*. Arcadia Publishing, Charleston, South Carolina. Page 8.

[7] U.S. Department of Agriculture, National Agricultural Statistics Service. "2014 State Agriculture Overview: Wyoming." http://www.nass.usda.gov/Quick_Stats/Ag_Overview/stateOverview.php?state=WYOMING

[8] Weidel, Nancy. *Images of America: Wyoming's Historic Ranches*. Arcadia Publishing, Charleston, South Carolina. Page 11.

[9] Weidel, Nancy. 2014. *Images of America: Wyoming's Historic Ranches*. Arcadia Publishing, Charleston, South Carolina. Page 19.

[10] Wyoming Tales and Trails. "Oil Camp Photos from Wyoming Tales and Trails: McFadden." http://www.wyomingtalesandtrails.com/mcfadden.html

[11] Wikipedia. "West Wendover, Nevada." https://en.wikipedia.org/wiki/West_Wendover,_Nevada

[12] Arrington, Leonard J., Thomas G. Alexander, and Charles Hibbard. "Historic Wendover Airfield: Preserving the Past – Educating the Future." http://www.wendoverairbase.com/world_war_2

Chapter 2

[1] Wood, Sterling A. Colonel, Colonel Edwin M. Van Bibber, Captain Thomas L. Lyons, PFC Robert G. Deihl. *History of the 313th Infantry in World War II*. Washington Infantry Journal Press. Page 15.

[2] Wood, Sterling A. Colonel, Colonel Edwin M. Van Bibber, Captain Thomas L. Lyons, PFC Robert G. Deihl. *History of the 313th Infantry in World War II*. Washington Infantry Journal Press. Page 17.

[3] Allen, Jaynet. *Camp Gruber: The War Years*. http://www.3riversmuseum.com/camp-gruber-the-war-years.html

[4] Kansas Historical Society. "Camp Phillips." In *The 808th Tank Destroyer Battalion*. http://www.808th.com/stateside/03c_phillips.htm

[5] Wood, Sterling A. Colonel, Colonel Edwin M. Van Bibber, Captain Thomas L. Lyons, PFC Robert G. Deihl. *History of the 313th Infantry in World War II*. Washington Infantry Journal Press. Page 45.

[6] Wood, Sterling A. Colonel, Colonel Edwin M. Van Bibber, Captain Thomas L. Lyons, PFC Robert G. Deihl. *History of the 313th Infantry in World War II*. Washington Infantry Journal Press. Page 52.

[7] Wood, Sterling A. Colonel, Colonel Edwin M. Van Bibber, Captain Thomas L. Lyons, PFC Robert G. Deihl. *History of the 313th Infantry in World War II*. Washington Infantry Journal Press. Page 48.

Chapter 3

[1] Wood, Sterling A. Colonel, Colonel Edwin M. Van Bibber, Captain Thomas L. Lyons, PFC Robert G. Deihl. *History of the 313th Infantry in World War II*. Washington Infantry Journal Press. Page 60.

[2] Wood, Sterling A. Colonel, Colonel Edwin M. Van Bibber, Captain Thomas L. Lyons, PFC Robert G. Deihl. *History of the 313th Infantry in World War II*. Washington Infantry Journal Press. Page 61.

[3] --. *79th Infantry Division*. http://www.history.army.mil/html/forcestruc/cbtchron/cc/079id.htm

[4] History.com Staff. "D-Day." http://www.history.com/topics/world-war-ii/d-day

[5] Wood, Sterling A. Colonel, Colonel Edwin M. Van Bibber, Captain Thomas L. Lyons, PFC Robert G. Deihl. *History of the 313th Infantry in World War II*. Washington Infantry Journal Press. Page 74.

[6] Zapotoczny, Walter S. *Breakout from the Hedgerows: A Lesson in Ingenuity*. http://www.militaryhistoryonline.com/wwii/articles/hedgerowbreakout.aspx

Chapter 4

[1] The History Place. *The History Place - The Defeat of Hitler: Battle of the Bulge*. http://www.historyplace.com/worldwar2/defeat/battle-bulge.htm

[2] Hart, James. "Sherman Tanks, Tiger Tanks & The Battle of the Bulge." http://warfarehistorynetwork.com/daily/wwii/sherman-tanks-tiger-tanks-the-battle-of-the-bulge/

[3] Andrews, Evan. *8 Things You May Not Know About the Battle of the Bulge*. http://www.history.com/news/8-things-you-may-not-know-about-the-battle-of-the-bulge

[4] History.com Staff. *The SS*. http://www.history.com/topics/world-war-ii/ss

Chapter 5

[1] The History Learning Site. *Field Marshal Bernard Montgomery*. http://www.historylearningsite.co.uk/world-war-two/military-commanders-of-world-war-two/field-marshal-bernard-montgomery/

2 Domes, Peter. *Task Force Baum: The Hammelburg Raid.* http://taskforcebaum.de/index1.html

Chapter 7

1 Wyoming Tales and Trails. "Lincoln Highway Photos." http://www.wyomingtalesandtrails.com/lincrockriv.html

2 Wikipedia. "Rock River, Wyoming." https://en.wikipedia.org/wiki/Rock_River,_Wyoming

3 Laramie Plains Museum at the Historic Ivinson Mansion. "History of the City of Laramie." http://www.laramiemuseum.org/historyofthecity.html

Chapter 8

1 Cooper, Craig. *A History of Water Law, Water Rights & Water Development in Wyoming 1868-2002.* http://wwdc.state.wy.us/history/Wyoming_Water_Law_History.pdf

2 Freudenrich, Craig, and Jonathan Strickland. "How Oil Drilling Works." In *How Stuff Works Science.* http://science.howstuffworks.com/environmental/energy/oil-drilling2.htm

3 U.S. Energy Information Administration. *U.S. States: State Profiles and Energy Estimates.* http://www.eia.gov/state/
4 U.S. Energy Information Administration. *Profile Analysis.* http://www.eia.gov/state/analysis.cfm?sid=WY

5 Wikipedia. "History of Wyoming: Mining." https://en.wikipedia.org/wiki/History_of_Wyoming#Mining

[6] Nickerson, Gregory. "Industry, Politics and Power: The Union Pacific in Wyoming."
http://www.wyohistory.org/essays/union-pacific-railroad

[7] Propst, Chris. "Rock Springs, Wyoming."
http://www.wyohistory.org/essays/rock-springs-wyoming

[8] Wikipedia. "History of rail transport in the United States."
https://en.wikipedia.org/wiki/History_of_rail_transport_in_the_United_States

[9] Andersen, Chamois L. "The Coal Business in Wyoming."
http://www.wyohistory.org/encyclopedia/coal-business-wyoming

[10] Wikipedia. "History of coal mining in the United States."
https://en.wikipedia.org/wiki/History_of_coal_mining_in_the_United_States

[11] Roberts, Phil. *Boom and Bust, Again: Wyoming in the 1970s*.
http://www.uwyo.edu/robertshistory/new_history_of_wyoming_chapter_19.htm

[12] U.S. Energy Information Administration. *Frequently Asked Questions*. http://www.eia.gov/tools/faqs/faq.cfm?id=69&t=2

[13] Roberts, Phil. "The Oil Business in Wyoming."
http://www.wyohistory.org/encyclopedia/oil-business-wyoming

[14] Petroleum Association of Wyoming. *Wyoming Oil and Gas Facts and Figures 2015 Edition*. http://www.pawyo.org/facts-figuers.pdf

[15] American Oil & Gas Historical Society. *First Wyoming Oil Well*. http://aoghs.org/newsletter/first-wyoming-oil-well/

[16] Roberts, Phil. "Chapter 9: History of Oil in Wyoming." In *Phil Roberts, A New History of Wyoming.* http://www.uwyo.edu/robertshistory/history_of_oil_in_wyoming.htm

[17] Chevron U.S.A. Inc., Commissioned by. *The Overthrust Industrial Association: A Public/Private Partnership History and Case Study.* http://www.sublettewyo.com/archives/42/Overthrust_Case_Study_1988%5B1%5D.pdf

[18] Noble, Ann Chambers. "The Jonah Field and Pinedale Anticline: A natural-gas success story." http://www.wyohistory.org/essays/jonah-field-and-pinedale-anticline-natural-gas-success-story#sthash.keuQSawx.dpuf

[19] Andersen, Chamois L., and Lori Van Pelt. "Wyoming's Uranium Drama: Risks, Rewards and Remorse." http://www.wyohistory.org/encyclopedia/wyomings-uranium-drama-risks-rewards-and-remorse#sthash.fGYrl7Zo.dpuf

[20] Wikipedia. "Uranium mining in the United States." https://en.wikipedia.org/wiki/Uranium_mining_in_the_United_States

[21] Mast, Tom. "Pumping Water to Powering Homes: Harnessing Wyoming's Wind." http://www.wyohistory.org/encyclopedia/wind-power#sthash.bqd6QamC.dpuf

[22] U.S. Department of the Interior Bureau of Land Management. "Split Estate Mineral Ownership." http://www.blm.gov/wy/st/en/programs/mineral_resources/split-estate.html

[23] U.S. Department of the Interior Bureau of Land Management. "Split Estate: Rights, Responsibilities, and Opportunities." http://www.blm.gov/style/medialib/blm/wo/MINERALS__RE ALTY__AND_RESOURCE_PROTECTION_/bmps.Par.5748 6.File.dat/SplitEstate07.pdf

Chapter 9

[1] Web Guides. "Primary Documents in American History: Morrill Act." http://www.loc.gov/rr/program/bib/ourdocs/Morrill.html

[2] Wikipedia. "Hatch Act of 1887." https://en.wikipedia.org/wiki/Hatch_Act_of_1887

[3] Oklahoma Agricultural Experiment Station. *Hatch Act of 1887*. http://oaes.okstate.edu/hatch-act

[4] Wikipedia. "Colorado State University." https://en.wikipedia.org/wiki/Colorado_State_University

[5] Colorado State University. "About Us." In College of Agricultural Sciences Agricultural Experiment Station. http://aes.agsci.colostate.edu/about-us/

[6] Colorado State University. "Nationally Known Pioneer in Equine Science and Veterinary Medicine to be Honored by Colorado State University." http://www.news.colostate.edu/Release/Print/1956

[7] Pickett, B.W. *Sex, Science, and Survival in Academe: A History of the Animal Reproduction and Biotechnology Laboratory at Colorado State University*. Animal Reproduction and Biotechnology Laboratory, Colorado State University, Fort Collins. Page 33.

[8] Pickett, B.W. *Sex, Science, and Survival in Academe: A History of the Animal Reproduction and Biotechnology Laboratory at Colorado State University*. Animal Reproduction and Biotechnology Laboratory, Colorado State University, Fort Collins. Page 34.

[9] --. "Recipient of the 2008 IETS Pioneer Award: George E. Seidel, Jr., PhD." http://www.iets.org/pdf/awards/2008PioneerSeidel_Citation.pd f

[10] Colorado State University. "George E. Seidel, Jr., PhD." http://csu-cvmbs.colostate.edu/academics/bms/Pages/george-seidel.aspx

[11] University of Wyoming. *The University of Wyoming: Founded in 1886*. http://www.uwyo.edu/anniversaries/history-of-uw/index.html

[12] University of Wyoming. *College Overview: College of Agriculture and Natural Resources*. http://www.uwyo.edu/uwag/college-overview/mission-statement.html

[13] ResearchGate. *James W. Waggoner*. https://www.researchgate.net/profile/James_Waggoner

Chapter 10

[1] Achilles Cattle Company. *The Sire that Started it All!!: Simmental : Breed for Milk, Fertility, Conformation: Achilles Cattle Company Sire Directory*. Leech Printing LTD., Brandon, Manitoba Canada. Page 10.

[2] Achilles Cattle Company. *The Sire that Started it All!!: Simmental : Breed for Milk, Fertility, Conformation: Achilles Cattle Company Sire Directory.* Leech Printing LTD., Brandon, Manitoba Canada. Page 5.

[3] --. *Agricultural Credit-Meaning, Definition, Need and Classification.* http://agridr.in/tnauEAgri/eagri50/AECO241/pdf/lec03.pdf

[4] Laramie Regional Airport. "About Us." http://www.laramieairport.com/about-us

[5] Wikipedia. Herbert J. Brees. https://en.wikipedia.org/wiki/Herbert_J._Brees

[6] Linse, Tamara. "An Audience Member Extraordinaire." http://www.uwyo.edu/uwyo/2012/13-2/douglas-reeves.html

BIBLIOGRAPHY

--. n.d. *Agricultural Credit-Meaning, Definition, Need and Classification.* <http://agridr.in/tnauEAgri/eagri50/AECO241/pdf/lec03.pdf>. Accessed August 2015.

--. n.d. *79th Infantry Division.* <http://www.history.army.mil/html/forcestruc/cbtchron/cc/079id.htm> Accessed August 2015.

--. n.d. "Recipient of the 2008 IETS Pioneer Award: George E. Seidel, Jr., PhD." *Reproduction, Fertility and Development,* 2008, 20, xxv. CSIRO Publishing. <http://www.iets.org/pdf/awards/2008PioneerSeidel_Citation.pdf>. Accessed August 2015.

Achilles Cattle Company. 1973. *The Sire that Started it All!!: Simmental : Breed for Milk, Fertility, Conformation : Achilles Cattle Company Sire Directory.* Leech Printing LTD., Brandon, Manitoba Canada.

Allen, Jaynet. n.d. *Camp Gruber: The War Years.* <http://www.3riversmuseum.com/camp-gruber-the-war-years.html>. Accessed March 18, 2015.

American Heritage Center. 2015. *Lance D. Robinson Scrapbook.* University of Wyoming, American Heritage Center, Lance D. Robinson scrapbook, Accession Number 12622. <http://digitalcollections.uwyo.edu:8180/luna/servlet/uwydbuwy~146~146>. Accessed August 2015.

_____. 2011. *W.B.D. and Annette B. Gray Papers*. University of Wyoming, American Heritage Center, W.B.D. and Annette B. Gray Papers, Accession Number 1053, Box 12. <ah01053_1460.jpg>. Accessed August 2015.

_____. 2011. *W.B.D. and Annette B. Gray Papers*. University of Wyoming, American Heritage Center, W.B.D. and Annette B. Gray Papers, Accession Number 1053, Box 13. <ah01053_1463.jpg>. Accessed August 2015.

_____. 2011. *J.S. Palen Collection*. University of Wyoming, American Heritage Center, J. S. Palen Collection, Accession Number 10472, Box 87, Folder 5. <ah10472_0784.jpg>. Accessed August 2015.

_____. 2011. *J.S. Palen Collection*. University of Wyoming, American Heritage Center, J. S. Palen Collection, Accession Number 10472, Box 88, Folder 13. <ah10472_1336.jpg> and <ah10472_1392>. Accessed August 2015.

American Oil & Gas Historical Society. n.d. *First Wyoming Oil Well*. <http://aoghs.org/newsletter/first-wyoming-oil-well/>. Accessed August 2015.

Andersen, Chamois L. n.d. "The Coal Business in Wyoming." WyoHistory.org. <http://www.wyohistory.org/encyclopedia/coal-business-wyoming>. Accessed August 2015.

Andersen, Chamois L., and Lori Van Pelt. n.d. "Wyoming's Uranium Drama: Risks, Rewards and Remorse." <http://www.wyohistory.org/encyclopedia/wyomings-uranium-drama-risks-rewards-and-remorse#sthash.fGYrl7Zo.dpuf>. WyoHistory.org. Accessed August 2015.

Andrews, Evan. 2014. *8 Things You May Not Know About the Battle of the Bulge*. <http://www.history.com/news/8-things-you-may-not-know-about-the-battle-of-the-bulge>. Accessed May 10, 2015.

Arrington, Leonard J., Thomas G. Alexander, and Charles Hibbard. n.d. "Historic Wendover Airfield: Preserving the Past – Educating the Future." <http://www.wendoverairbase.com/world_war_2>. Accessed August 2015.

Chevron U.S.A. Inc., Commissioned by. n.d. *The Overthrust Industrial Association: A Public/Private Partnership History and Case Study*. <http://www.sublettewyo.com/archives/42/Overthrust_Case_Study_1988%5B1%5D.pdf>. Accessed August 2015.

Colorado State University. 2000. "Nationally Known Pioneer in Equine Science and Veterinary Medicine to be Honored by Colorado State University." <http://www.news.colostate.edu/Release/Print/1956>. Accessed August 2015.

Colorado State University. n.d. "About Us." In *College of Agricultural Sciences Agricultural Experiment Station*. <http://aes.agsci.colostate.edu/about-us/>. Accessed August 2015.

Colorado State University. n.d. "George E. Seidel, Jr., PhD." In Department of Biomedical Sciences College of Veterinary Medicine & Biomedical Sciences. <http://csu-cvmbs.colostate.edu/academics/bms/Pages/george-seidel.aspx>. Accessed August 2015.

Cooper, Craig. 2004. *A History of Water Law, Water Rights & Water Development in Wyoming 1868-2002.* <http://wwdc.state.wy.us/history/Wyoming_Water_Law_Histo ry.pdf>. Accessed August 2015.

Domes, Peter. 2002. *Task Force Baum: The Hammelburg Raid.* <http://taskforcebaum.de/index1.html>. Accessed June 7, 2015.

Eisenhower, John S.D. 1969. *The Bitter Woods: The Battle of the Bulge.* Da Capo Press.

Freudenrich, Craig, and Jonathan Strickland. n.d. "How Oil Drilling Works." In *How Stuff Works Science.* <http://science.howstuffworks.com/environmental/energy/oil-drilling2.htm>. Accessed August 2015.

Gilbert, Martin. 1989. *The Second World War.* Holt Paperbacks. Henry Holt and Company, LLC, New York, New York.

Hart, James. 2014. "Sherman Tanks, Tiger Tanks & The Battle of the Bulge." *Warfare History Network.* <http://warfarehistorynetwork.com/daily/wwii/sherman-tanks-tiger-tanks-the-battle-of-the-bulge/>. Accessed August 9, 2015.

History.com Staff. 2009. *D-Day.* <http://www.history.com/topics/world-war-ii/d-day>. A+E Networks. Accessed May 9, 2015.

_____. 2009. *The SS.* <http://www.history.com/topics/world-war-ii/ss>. A+E Networks. Accessed May 11, 2015.

The History Learning Site. 2014. *Field Marshal Bernard Montgomery*. <http://www.historylearningsite.co.uk/world-war-two/military-commanders-of-world-war-two/field-marshal-bernard-montgomery/>. Accessed August 2015.

The History Place. 2010. *The History Place - The Defeat of Hitler*: *Battle of the Bulge*. <http://www.historyplace.com/worldwar2/defeat/battle-bulge.htm>. Accessed May 10, 2015.

Kansas Historical Society. n.d. "Camp Phillips." *The 808th Tank Destroyer Battalion*. <http://www.808th.com/stateside/03c_phillips.htm>. Accessed March 18, 2015.

Laramie Plains Museum at the Historic Ivinson Mansion. n.d. "History of the City of Laramie." <http://www.laramiemuseum.org/historyofthecity.html>. Accessed August 2015.

Laramie Regional Airport. n.d. "About Us." <http://www.laramieairport.com/about-us>. Accessed August 2015.

Linse, Tamara. 2012. "An Audience Member Extraordinaire." *UWyo Magazine*, Volume 13, Number 2, January 2012. <http://www.uwyo.edu/uwyo/2012/13-2/douglas-reeves.html>. Accessed August 2015.

Mast, Tom. n.d. "Pumping Water to Powering Homes: Harnessing Wyoming's Wind." WyoHistory.org. <http://www.wyohistory.org/encyclopedia/wind-power#sthash.bqd6QamC.dpuf>. Accessed August 2015.

Nickerson, Gregory. n.d. "Industry, Politics and Power: The Union Pacific in Wyoming." WyoHistory.org. <http://www.wyohistory.org/essays/union-pacific-railroad>. Accessed August 2015.

Noble, Ann Chambers. n.d. "The Jonah Field and Pinedale Anticline: A natural-gas success story." WyoHistory.org. <http://www.wyohistory.org/essays/jonah-field-and-pinedale-anticline-natural-gas-success-story#sthash.keuQSawx.dpuf>. Accessed August 2015.

Petroleum Association of Wyoming. 2015. *Wyoming Oil and Gas Facts and Figures 2015 Edition.* <http://www.pawyo.org/facts-figuers.pdf>. Accessed August 2015.

Pickett, B.W. 2012. *Sex, Science, and Survival in Academe: A History of the Animal Reproduction and Biotechnology Laboratory at Colorado State University.* Animal Reproduction and Biotechnology Laboratory, Colorado State University, Fort Collins.

Propst, Chris. n.d. "Rock Springs, Wyoming." WyoHistory.org. <http://www.wyohistory.org/essays/rock-springs-wyoming>. Accessed August 2015.

Roberts, Phil. n.d. *Boom and Bust, Again: Wyoming in the 1970s.* <http://www.uwyo.edu/robertshistory/new_history_of_wyoming_chapter_19.htm>. Accessed August 2015.

Roberts, Phil. n.d. "Chapter 9: History of Oil in Wyoming." In *Phil Roberts, A New History of Wyoming.* <http://www.uwyo.edu/robertshistory/history_of_oil_in_wyoming.htm>. Accessed August 2015.

Roberts, Phil. n.d. "The Oil Business in Wyoming."
WyoHistory.org.
<http://www.wyohistory.org/encyclopedia/oil-business-
wyoming>. Accessed August 2015.

U.S. Department of Agriculture, National Agricultural
Statistics Service. 2015. "2014 State Agriculture Overview:
Wyoming."
<http://www.nass.usda.gov/Quick_Stats/Ag_Overview/stateOv
erview.php?state=WYOMING> Accessed August 2015.

U.S. Department of the Interior Bureau of Land Management.
2012. "Split Estate Mineral Ownership."
<http://www.blm.gov/wy/st/en/programs/mineral_resources/spl
it-estate.html>. Accessed August 2015.

U.S. Department of the Interior Bureau of Land Management.
2007. "Split Estate: Rights, Responsibilities, and
Opportunities."
<http://www.blm.gov/style/medialib/blm/wo/MINERALS__R
EALTY__AND_RESOURCE_PROTECTION_/bmps.Par.574
86.File.dat/SplitEstate07.pdf>. Accessed August 2015.

U.S. Energy Information Administration. n.d. *Frequently
Asked Questions.*
<http://www.eia.gov/tools/faqs/faq.cfm?id=69&t=2>.
Accessed August 2015.

U.S. Energy Information Administration. n.d. *Profile Analysis.*
<http://www.eia.gov/state/analysis.cfm?sid=WY>. Accessed
August 2015.

U.S. Energy Information Administration. n.d. *U.S. States: State
Profiles and Energy Estimates.* <http://www.eia.gov/state/>.
Accessed August 2015.

Web Guides. n.d. "Primary Documents in American History: Morrill Act." <http://www.loc.gov/rr/program/bib/ourdocs/Morrill.html>. Accessed August 2015.

Weidel, Nancy. 2014. *Images of America: Wyoming's Historic Ranches*. Arcadia Publishing, Charleston, South Carolina. Wikipedia. n.d. "Colorado State University." <https://en.wikipedia.org/wiki/Colorado_State_University>. Accessed August 2015.

_____. n.d. "Hatch Act of 1887." <https://en.wikipedia.org/wiki/Hatch_Act_of_1887>. Accessed August 2015.

_____. n.d. "Herbert J. Brees." <https://en.wikipedia.org/wiki/Herbert_J._Brees>. Accessed August 2015.

_____. n.d. "History of coal mining in the United States." <https://en.wikipedia.org/wiki/History_of_coal_mining_in_the_United_States>. Accessed August 2015.

_____. n.d. "History of rail transport in the United States." <https://en.wikipedia.org/wiki/History_of_rail_transport_in_the_United_States>. Accessed August 2015.

_____. n.d. "History of Wyoming: Mining." <https://en.wikipedia.org/wiki/History_of_Wyoming#Mining>. Accessed August 2015.

_____. n.d. "Rock River, Wyoming." <https://en.wikipedia.org/wiki/Rock_River,_Wyoming>. Accessed August 2015.

_____. n.d. "Uranium mining in the United States."
<https://en.wikipedia.org/wiki/Uranium_mining_in_the_Unite
d_States>. Accessed August 2015.

_____. n.d. "West Wendover, Nevada."
<https://en.wikipedia.org/wiki/West_Wendover,_Nevada>
Accessed August 9, 2015.

_____. n.d. "Winter of 1886–87."
<https://en.wikipedia.org/wiki/Winter_of_1886%E2%80%938
7>. Accessed August 2015.

Wood, Sterling A. Colonel, Colonel Edwin M. Van Bibber,
Captain Thomas L. Lyons, PFC Robert G. Deihl. 1947. *History
of the 313th Infantry in World War II*. Washington Infantry
Journal Press.

Wyoming Tales and Trails. n.d. "Oil Camp Photos from
Wyoming Tales and Trails: McFadden."
<http://www.wyomingtalesandtrails.com/mcfadden.html>.
Accessed March 24, 2015.

_____. n.d. "Lincoln Highway Photos."
<http://www.wyomingtalesandtrails.com/lincrockriv.html>.
Accessed August 2015.

Zapotoczny, Walter S. 2005. *Breakout from the Hedgerows: A
Lesson in Ingenuity*.
<http://www.militaryhistoryonline.com/wwii/articles/hedgerow
breakout.aspx>. MilitaryHistoryOnline.com. Accessed March
19, 2015.

Made in the USA
Monee, IL
27 May 2020